His Hallowed Name
Revealed Again

Keith E. Johnson

BIBLICAL FOUNDATIONS ACADEMY

Minneapolis, Minnesota
2011

A BIBLICAL FOUNDATIONS ACADEMY BOOK

PUBLISHING HISTORY

For His Name's Sake
Hardcover Edition, 2003

His Hallowed Name Revealed Again
Spiral Bound Study and Perfect Bound Paperback, First Edition, 2010
Perfect Bound Paperback, Second Edition, 2011

EPUB Edition, Digital Book, 2011

MINNEAPOLIS, MINNESOTA

ISBN 978-0-615-33323-6

Copies of this book can be obtained at
www.hishallowedname.com

Write us at:
BIBLICAL FOUNDATIONS ACADEMY
3348 Park Avenue
Minneapolis, Minnesota 55407

Contact us via e-mail: info@biblicalfoundationsacademy.com

Scripture teaches us in Psalms 122:4 that we are to
"Give thanks to the name יהוה."
It is with great thanks that I dedicate this book to His name
יהוה.

CONTENTS

AUTHOR'S NOTE

I encourage the reader to compare the Scripture references that I have cited with two or more established translations, in particular the New American Standard Bible, New International Version, Revised Standard Version, King James Version, or another translation of your choice. My hope and prayer is that you will be like the people of Berea who . . .

> . . . examined the Scriptures daily to see whether these things were so.
>
> ACTS 17:11

Scripture quotes are based on the New American Standard Bible (NASB) unless otherwise noted.

Special acknowledgment. In the spring of 2002 I met Nehemia Gordon in Jerusalem, Israel. Nehemia holds a Master's Degree in Biblical Studies and a Bachelor's Degree in Archeology from the Hebrew University in Jerusalem. Nehemia has worked as a translator of the Dead Sea Scrolls and as a researcher deciphering ancient Hebrew manuscripts. As a result of spending time with him touring the Old City of Jerusalem and discussing the Hebrew Bible, we crafted a relationship that started me on the path of using my Hebrew Bible for more than just a reference tool. Over the last several years Nehemia has shared invaluable study tools that have allowed me to dig deeply into the Hebrew Scriptures. I especially want to acknowledge his help in teaching me a system for studying my Hebrew Bible and for helping me gain access to information from historical sources that normally would have been inaccessible to me. Nehemia has also been gracious enough to let me incorporate some portions of his hitherto unpublished study on the Divine Name into this work, especially some of the technical linguistic explanations.

FOREWORD

In the summer of 2009 Keith Johnson phoned me and told me he had written a study on the name of our Heavenly Father. He asked if I would read it and give my feedback, but I said I was too busy to read his "little study." Over the next few months, whenever we met or spoke he would ask me to read it, and I always had an excuse as to why I was too busy to read the "little study." I became so used to calling it the "little study" that I referred to it this way during a television interview we did the following year. Now, after finally reading *His Hallowed Name Revealed Again,* I can confidently call it a monumental masterpiece that honors our Heavenly Father by honoring and proclaiming His eternal name. This "little study" that you, the reader, are about to embark on has already had a profound impact on my life in a most unexpected way.

It happened while Keith and I were on a speaking tour of South Africa for our joint book, *A Prayer to Our Father: Hebrew Origins of the Lord's Prayer.* In the months leading up to the tour, the promoter asked us to prepare a list of sites we wanted to visit. After giving it much thought, I told her I wanted nothing more than to teach the word of God, and would rather squeeze more speaking venues into our tight schedule than spend time sightseeing. For his part, Keith had his heart set on visiting two places: Kruger National Park and Robben Island. When we arrived in Johannesburg and learned that our scheduled trip to Kruger National Park had been canceled, Keith took it rather well. He explained to me that although he had always wanted to go to the park, the place that was *really* important to him was Robben Island, where Nelson Mandela had been imprisoned during his struggle against apartheid.

Later that week we arrived in Cape Town. The promoter met us at the airport and drove us to a scenic spot on the coast where in the distance we could see the dreaded Robben Island, surrounded by the cold, harsh waters of Table Bay. It came as a shock to both of us when she informed us we would not, after all, be able to visit the island. There was a long waiting list and she had not ordered tickets in time. At that moment I saw something change in Keith. We had done everything else we had planned, speaking throughout the country, but Robben Island was the one place Keith wanted to go more than anywhere else. He now became a man on a mission. Even before the Robben Island incident, Keith had told me it bothered him that most of the people who came to our presentations were middle-class, educated folks. He desperately wanted to go out into the townships and interact with the people who comprise the vast majority of the South African population. To say the least, I was quite resistant to the idea. It was not part of our scheduled itinerary, and every time Keith brought it up I objected that we simply did not have time. Earlier in the tour I had made the mistake of drinking tap water, so I was in no condition to venture into one of these townships; furthermore, we had been warned they were very dangerous. After the Robben Island debacle, nothing could have kept Keith out of the townships. The only question was whether I would go with him.

From Cape Town we drove three and a half hours to speak in a small farming community. After our presentation we trekked into the countryside down a series of dirt roads for some fellowship at a farm owned by our local host, who happened to be an Englishman married to a Jewish woman. I remember sitting on the sofa, struggling with another bout of what Americans call "Montezuma's Revenge." (During my time in South Africa I came to refer to it as Shaka Zulu's Revenge.) Keith was at the dining room table talking to our host about how he wanted to visit a township somewhere in the area before our flight out of Cape Town the next morning. Since we were three and a half hours from the airport, I was sure our host would try to convince Keith how frivolous this mission would be in such a limited timeframe. To my surprise the man said, "I know someone in one of the townships just outside of Cape Town, on the way to the airport. Shall I give him a call and arrange a meeting?" My eyes almost popped out of my head, and I moaned that I was too sick to go. Keith was undeterred and demanded more details. Our host explained that the man he knew in the Khayelitsha Township was the pastor of a small church. He had met the pastor years earlier when he helped him lay the bricks for his church. When the man said Khayelitsha, all the locals fell silent and gave each other awkward looks. The silence was broken by a heavyset woman with a strong Afrikaans accent who grew up in Cape Town. She shouted: "Khayelitsha! You can't go to Khayelitsha! You just walk in there and they *kill* you!" This only encouraged Keith. A few minutes later he was on the phone with the pastor of the small brick church in Khayelitsha, and a meeting was set for early the next morning. We realized we had to drive back to Cape Town that night in order to meet the pastor and still reach the airport on time. We arrived in Cape Town after midnight, and I fell asleep while Keith planned our excursion to the township.

Early that morning we drove to the entrance of Khayelitsha, where we were to meet the pastor. Khayelitsha is a sprawling shanty-town full of tin-roofed, wooden shacks and outhouses, with a population of more than 400,000. The main road was paved but a labyrinth of smaller dirt roads and alleyways branched off it. We were told not to venture into the township by ourselves since we easily could turn down a wrong alley and get lost, which might prove to be fatal. After waiting for what seemed like an eternity, the pastor met us and we followed him to his church.

The church was a simple brick building with a single, large prayer hall and some small rooms in the back. The pastor explained how various people had donated the bricks and the mortar and even the labor to construct it all. As he talked, his wife and some of his children came out of one of the back rooms, where they all lived. The pastor told us about himself and his church, then he asked us to tell him about ourselves. I told him I was born in the United States but have lived in Jerusalem, Israel, since 1993. The pastor interrupted me and asked if I spoke Hebrew. I told him that of course I did. When he heard this he began to bounce up and down in excitement, and then turned to me and said in his thick African accent: "About seven years ago I had a dream, and in that dream I saw four letters." He explained that although he did not know any Hebrew, he had always believed the four letters to be Hebrew letters. He was very excited to meet a Hebrew-speaking person and hoped I could help him understand what he had seen in the dream.

The first thing that most English-speakers think of when they hear about a four-letter word is some sort of profanity. But as a Hebrew-speaker, the first thing I thought of was the name of our Heavenly Father, written with the four Hebrew consonants *Yod-He-Vav-He*. In Hebrew, this is often referred to as "the four-letter name" (*shem ben dalet otiot*). In English it is called the Tetragrammaton, from the Greek *tetra,* meaning "four," and *grammaton,* meaning "letters." My mind started to race as I wondered if this African pastor, who knew no Hebrew, really could have seen the name *Yod-He-Vav-He* in a dream.

I asked him if he could write the letters for me. He shook his head and told me that his native language was Xhosa; his tongue made a little click when he said "Xhosa." He then told me he had learned English as his second language 10 years earlier when he came to Khayelitsha. Despite mastering these two languages, he had no idea how to write Hebrew. I then asked him to bring me a pen and paper. He shouted something to his wife in what I assumed to be Xhosa, and in a few moments his little boy came out of the back room with a single sheet of paper. The pastor handed me a pencil and I bent over, using my thigh as a writing surface, as I wrote out the four letters of the name: *Yod-He-Vav-He*. Holding up the paper, I asked him if the letters I wrote were what he saw in his dream. He looked at the paper, cocked his head to the side, and hesitantly said that it sort of looked like what he saw in the dream, but he could not be sure. As he explained this, he actually wrote the letters in the air. He must have been doing this unconsciously, but I was fairly certain he wrote *Yod-He-Vav-He* with his air-letters.

Keith had been quiet the whole time I spoke to the pastor about the dream, but evidently decided it was time to get involved. He looked over my shoulder at the paper and then gave me that quintessential "Keith look," the one that expresses a four-letter *English* word without actually saying it. He pointed at my letters and exclaimed: "Nehemia, I can barely read what you wrote, and I read Hebrew! How can you expect him to make out your chicken scratches?" I have to admit, I've always had bad penmanship; my teachers in school never stopped complaining about it. Keith walked out of the church without saying a word and returned a few minutes later with a copy of *His Hallowed Name Revealed Again*. Since first asking me to read it, the "little study" had undergone several revisions and was now a 175-page, spiral-bound book with a striking color cover. The four letters of the name of our Heavenly Father were emblazoned on the cover in beautifully printed Hebrew: יהוה (*Yod-He-Vav-He*). He showed the book to the pastor, who exclaimed without hesitation: "That is what I saw! Those were the four letters!"

At this point I need to stop and share something about myself. Both my parents are Jews of Lithuanian extraction, known as "Litvaks." The Litvaks have traditionally been considered the intellectual elite of the Jewish world. Ask any Litvak and he'll tell you this reputation is well-deserved, earned through centuries of book learning and study. Part of my upbringing as a Litvak Jew was to distrust anything deemed "too spiritual;" dreams and miracles were best left to the realm of folk superstition. When the Xhosa pastor started to tell me about his dream, my natural reaction was skepticism. In fact, if I had not been there and seen the look on his face when he saw the four letters on the cover of *His Hallowed Name Revealed Again,* I probably would not put much stock in what happened. But I saw the look on his face and have no doubt that he recognized something he had seen before. At the same time, I struggled to process what I was witnessing. Everything in my training and upbringing taught me that God does not reveal His name in dreams to Christian pastors in shanty-towns. This was not consistent with the box I had created for God. Seeing the look on the pastor's face when he recognized those four letters, the Litvak in me was shouting, "God! What are you doing? Get back in your box!" One thing I have learned from my adventures with Keith is that our Heavenly Father is far bigger than the manmade boxes we have created for Him.

After the incident in Khayelitsha I gave a great deal of thought to what happened. I thought about how God revealed His name to a Xhosa pastor in a dream, knowing this man would never be able to decipher it by himself. I also realized that although I had the Litvak erudition, I did not have the dream. God knew it would take both the knowledge and the dream—both the information and the inspiration—to reveal His name.

What happened in Khayelitsha is a snapshot of what Keith Johnson has done with the eternal name of our Heavenly Father. He has carefully examined the erudition of Jewish scribes who for centuries have preserved for the entire world the consonants, vowels, and accents of the Hebrew Bible in two key manuscripts: the Aleppo Codex and the Leningrad Codex. The Aleppo Codex is considered so important that it is the *only* manuscript displayed alongside the Dead Sea Scrolls at the *Shrine of the Book* in Israel's national museum in Jerusalem. The Leningrad Codex is considered the second most important Hebrew manuscript, and serves as the textual basis of the printed Bible used in every seminary and university in the world. During Keith's visit to Israel last month we had the opportunity to confirm the validity of a third witness: the *Cairo Codex of the Prophets*. In this "little study" Keith takes the information from these sacred manuscripts, combines it with God-given inspiration, and produces a compelling witness to the importance, meaning, and pronunciation of the name of the Creator of the universe. *Hallelu YAH!*

Nehemia Gordon
Jerusalem, Israel
March 2011

PREFACE

This book is my *second* attempt at releasing the fire of the revelation of His name so it might illuminate and warm those who want to see and experience it for themselves. In 2003 I wrote *For His Name's Sake,*[1] a private study to explain to a close circle of influence the transformation that had resulted from my journey to Jerusalem the previous year, where I first encountered His hallowed name. Since then, that information has become inspiration and has gone through a refining process I never could have imagined.

In the summer of 2009, after the release of *A Prayer to Our Father: Hebrew Origins of the Lord's Prayer* which Nehemia Gordon and I co-authored, I decided there was much more to say about the phrase "hallowed be your name." I fasted, prayed, and rewrote my first study. It was invigorating to venture back into the process of writing about this glorious name. This time I introduced the information in phases. After a small group of people in Charlotte reviewed the manuscript, I gave it to 100 people from around the United States who agreed to go through the study and offer comments. Then I sought public input from around the world through a limited-edition version. I am humbled to report that people from a wide range of religious, ethnic, and socio-economic backgrounds requested nearly 500 copies!

As a reflection of my desire for this message to span the globe, I have included the following testimonies from eight different parts of the world! I have been amazed at the depth of many responses to this information. It is clear to me that there is a remnant of people who are ready for His hallowed name to be revealed again!

> I don't know where to start. *His Hallowed Name Revealed Again* is so important! I think this study of yours is a great breakthrough, and I know there are

---

[1] Johnson, Keith E. *For His Name's Sake.* North Carolina: Biblical Foundations Press, 2003.
[2] Shavuot is a biblical holy day that is celebrated on the fiftieth day after Passover (Leviticus

many others out there that the Father is drawing that will eat it up! The CD is a great worship tool, and I believe that there is power in speaking out the Hebrew. Any layman can follow right through and understand it. You have a very "folksy" style that makes it very personal.

Miri Burgin – Jerusalem, Israel

I just received a copy of your book *His Hallowed Name Revealed Again* yesterday. I couldn't put it down. I think you have resolved the sacred name issue with top-notch scholarship. I've been reading the Hebrew Bible for forty-five years, and had come to the same conclusions as a matter of familiarity. I'm associate professor of comparative religion at the University of Stockholm since 1982 (oavlönad docent in Swedish).

Thomas McElwain – Kuopio, Finland

Calling Him by name makes Him ours and, even more important, it has made us His again. Prayers are no longer repetitive and almost a mantra, but now we put more thought into who it is that we are talking to. Not only His name but the qualities that accompany Him have replaced LORD, lord, Lord, Señor, HaShem, and other common names we have been giving to our Father. Can't wait to give it another look and see how this book can bless our country and our continent, which has been deprived of the many blessings of calling our Father and King by name.

Ricardo and Vanessa Flores – Caracas, Venezuela

Thank you so much for this wonderful study. I want to run and proclaim this truth to all. Let His name be exalted among the nations and praised among the peoples!

Miryam – Stony Hill, Jamaica

What a blessing! I knew a bit on the name, but you gave me so many *wow* moments that I realized I had only seen the tip of the iceberg. Keith, thank you for blessing my life and the many that will read this study of yours.

Andrew Hodkinson – Durban, South Africa

I wanted so to tell you how the study has delighted me. Besides the abundant evidence you've presented, even the *sound* of the name is so much more pleasing and satisfying to the ear.

Janice Humphrey – Ontario, Canada

After being involved in Christianity for 30 years, the vast contents of what you are about to read was subtly concealed from us. It wasn't until we had the privilege of reading this valuable book that we gave our first serious study to the sacred Name of our Creator. Be prepared to be challenged as Keith Johnson reveals ancient Hebrew documents that unlock essential Scripture, so that you too may know and speak His hallowed Name revealed again!

Jono and Christine Vandor – Cootamundra, Australia

I read your new study *His Hallowed Name Revealed Again* and I can only say I was very impressed with the depth of the research, in-depth analysis, time, and dedication you invested in bringing this new revelation to us. I pastor a Shabbat-keeping and Messianic ministry. As the Igbo of Nigeria would say, "Onye a na akpo oku, mara aha ya!" This means "The person whose name you are calling knows his own name!"

Paul Onovoh – Atlanta, Georgia

I want to take this opportunity to thank all my study partners from around the world who have testified to how this information has ignited them to become ambassadors of His hallowed name. You can view more of their comments at www.hishallowedname.com. I also thank those who offered suggestions on content, grammar, design, and the instructional CD. I am humbled by their interest in this project and wish to express my deepest gratitude. I pray that He blesses them all abundantly!

וְהָלְכוּ עַמִּים רַבִּים וְאָמְרוּ לְכוּ וְנַעֲלֶה אֶל הַר יְהוָה

And many peoples will come and say, "Come, let us go up to the mountain of יהוה."

ISAIAH 2:3

א

ALEPH

CHAPTER ONE

CLOSE ENCOUNTERS

As a result of certain significant events in my life, I came to understand that I was being prepared for a life-changing journey to encounter His hallowed name. In the spring of 2002 I traveled to Jerusalem, Israel, in response to what I believed to be an invitation from our Heavenly Father to an appointment on earth. The time of the meeting was set for the biblical holy day of Shavuot/Pentecost.[2] What I encountered radically changed my life, my family, and my ministry. Until recently I kept most of what happened at that meeting private. Before I could share it publicly, I felt compelled to take the time necessary to better understand who our Heavenly Father is according to His word and who I am called to be according to His will. I am now ready.

---

[2] Shavuot is a biblical holy day that is celebrated on the fiftieth day after Passover (Leviticus 23:15–22). According to the second chapter of Acts, Pentecost commemorates the outpouring of the Holy Spirit upon the apostles and pilgrims who traveled to Jerusalem for Shavuot. This is the only festival that both Jews and Christians jointly acknowledge and celebrate.

Before my trip to Jerusalem, I had traveled to the top of Pike's Peak near Colorado Springs in 2001. As I stood on the top of the mountain on a clear day where I could see for what seemed like hundreds of miles in every direction, I prayed the most radical prayer of my life: "Father, teach me to love what you love and hate what you hate."

At that moment the great Maestro in heaven raised His hands and prepared to conduct a beautiful symphony in my life. I began to see and understand His will and His word in a new way. I could not get enough of the things He loved, and I could not stand the things He hated. I found myself looking for my identity in Him more than trying to find my significance in society.

Eventually a passage in Scripture gave me the freedom and confidence to walk the path He was laying out for me. In fact, it freed me from having to explain why a United Methodist pastor would be so keenly interested in His hallowed name. Neither do I have to force my encounters in Israel into a claim of Jewish blood. It would be impossible to produce records from either side of my family to connect me to one of the tribes of Israel. However, I am privileged to embrace all that my Heavenly Father offers to His children. Here is a portion of the passage that started me on my journey:

> Also the foreigners who join themselves to יהוה, to minister to Him, and to love the name יהוה, to be His servants, everyone who keeps from profaning the Sabbath and holds fast My covenant; even those I will bring to My holy mountain and make them joyful in My house of prayer.
>
> ISAIAH 56:6–7

I am a foreigner with no known Israelites in the family tree. Yet my Heavenly Father invited me to join myself to Him, to minister to Him, and to *love His name*. I could not resist. Over the following year I began to study His word as never before. I wanted to know everything I could about the language, history, and culture of my most prized possession: my Bible. I didn't realize until recently that the invitation in Isaiah was related to my appointment on His holy mountain in Israel.

What I find very encouraging as well as revelatory is that I experienced three encounters that continue to mold and shape me from the inside out. The preacher inside of me wants to say it like this: I encountered His time, His Torah, and His Tetragrammaton.[3] Since then I have learned the biblical precedent for my experience. When the people of Israel were delivered from Egypt, they encountered His time, His Torah, and his Tetragrammaton.[4] Likewise, Isaiah 56:6-7 encourages the foreigners who join themselves to יהוה to also encounter His time, His Torah, and His Tetragrammaton—His hallowed name. Amazing.

I wrote about some of this life-changing revelation in *A Prayer to Our Father: Hebrew Origins of the Lord's Prayer.* I had been studying with my co-author, Nehemia Gordon, for several years. Our ground-breaking study on the ancient prayer taught by the one called *Jesus/Yeshua* has been well received by many people of faith from around the world. One of the chapters in the book addresses the well-known English phrase "hallowed be thy name." In the Hebrew language, this phrase means "your name be sanctified." These four words in both the English and Hebrew versions connect to the single most important revelation I received while in Jerusalem: the meaning and pronunciation of the four Hebrew letters of His hallowed name.

I will never forget that amazing day. Come with me. As Nehemia and I waited to tour the tunnels under Jerusalem, I asked him a question that had intrigued me for a long time: How do you say the name of our Heavenly Father? I had asked this question of many Jewish people before Nehemia, but with no success. They

---

[3] The Tetragrammaton is the technical term for the four Hebrew letters that represent the name of our Heavenly Father. These four Hebrew letters are represented on the front cover of this book.

[4] See Exodus 12:1-2 and Exodus 19:1 regarding His time, Exodus 20:1-17 for His Torah, and Exodus 3 and 20:1 for His Tetragrammaton.

either said it was too holy to pronounce, too profound for me to understand, or too powerful for me to handle; therefore, I was prohibited from proclaiming His name. When I asked my new friend Nehemia, who happened to be both Jewish and a Hebrew Bible scholar, about the pronunciation of the name he responded by asking me a question: "Do you know any Hebrew?"

During the year prior to my trip to Israel, I had reacquainted myself with my Hebrew language studies from seminary. I was excited to respond to his question with a "Yes." After writing the four Hebrew letters יהוה on a piece of paper, Nehemia went on to give me a short refresher lesson on Hebrew vowels. After his discourse, I asked him to pronounce the name. With no hesitation he said something like, "According to the consonants and vowels found in the earliest vocalized Hebrew manuscripts, His name is pronounced . . ."[5]

Immediately it seemed as if all sights and sounds around us were frozen in time, like a freeze frame of a movie. I looked up and saw a man with a prayer shawl draped over his shoulders standing in front of us, a shofar[6] pressed to his lips. The moment Nehemia said the name, the man sent forth two blasts from his shofar. The freeze frame vanished. The pronunciation of the Heavenly Father's name, combined with the sound of the shofar, reverberated in my ears and revived my heart.

> While I was overcome with emotion at hearing a Jew pronounce the name followed by the blasts of the ram's horn, I needed to see the name for myself. So I put on my poker face, looked Nehemia straight in the eyes, and demanded that he show me where I could see the name written out in the Hebrew text of Scripture with the exact vowels he had just used. He explained that there were many such examples in the

---

[5] Vocalized means that the manuscript includes vowels so that each word can be pronounced when read.

[6] The shofar is a ram's horn that is blown on special occasions throughout the year.

oldest vocalized manuscripts of the Hebrew Bible. However, he could not remember book, chapter, and verse off the top of his head.[7]

After my movie-like experience was over, I asked Nehemia every question I could think of about the name יהוה. I felt like I was starving inside a buffet restaurant with no money to buy anything to eat. I'd had access to this life-changing name within the Hebrew Bible I had owned since seminary, and yet I didn't have the key to open the treasure chest that was within its pages. When I settled in my room for the night, I became a man on a mission. I opened my Hebrew Bible, which happened to be based on one of the very manuscripts Nehemia referenced, and began in the first verse of Genesis reading every single Hebrew letter one-by-one. I was looking for a four-letter word with three vowels and an accent.

Even though Nehemia is a Hebrew Bible scholar and translator of the Dead Sea Scrolls, his words were not enough. Hearing the name pronounced in concert with two blasts of a shofar was an astounding experience, yet I still was not satisfied. Though time was passing into the wee hours of the morning, I felt like I was still sitting across from the Western Wall in the beautiful Jerusalem morning air. Every time my eyes would see a י (yod) and then a ה (hey), I would slow down to see if it was the four-letter name with three vowels and an accent.

I still remember what seemed like looking for a needle in a haystack for hours. Then I saw it. Eureka! My eyes stayed fixed on the page as though I were looking at a million dollar lottery ticket while hearing my winning number called. I could hardly contain myself. I was looking at the name of our Heavenly Father in my Hebrew Bible from seminary, written so it could be pronounced just the way I heard it in Jerusalem. I'd had the name in my possession for ten years and never knew it was on my library shelf.

---

[7] N. Gordon and K. Johnson. *A Prayer to Our Father: Hebrew Origins of the Lord's Prayer.* Hilkiah Press, 2009, page 100.

I had come face to face with the pronunciation of four Hebrew letters combined with three vowels which answered the question that had burned in my mind and heart for so long: What is the name that is to be *hallowed* (sanctified)? These four Hebrew letters sparked a small personal flame in me. Over the next several years I huddled close to the light from this fire and shared the warmth of His name with family and friends.

The publication and subsequent book tour of *A Prayer to Our Father: Hebrew Origins of the Lord's Prayer* stoked this private campfire into a public bonfire. It seemed that every time I prayed, preached, or proclaimed "Your name be sanctified," the fire grew inside of me. I experienced what is described by the prophet Jeremiah:

> But if I say, "I will not remember Him or speak anymore in His name," then in my heart it becomes like a burning fire shut up in my bones; and I am weary of holding it in, and I cannot endure it.
> JEREMIAH 20:9

His Hallowed Name Revealed Again incorporates what I have learned over the last several years on the amazing topic of His name. This book presents an opportunity for interested people to inquire, inspect, and be inspired by incredible information about the perfect and *hallowed* name of our Heavenly Father. My prayer is that my attempt to present this information will motivate you to proclaim, pray, and praise His exalted, glorified, and sanctified name. My prayer will be answered if by the end of this book you learn, as I have,

to fear [revere] this honored and awesome name . . .
DEUTERONOMY 28:58

For those who would like to see the name that ignited the fire in me, here it is written in an ancient Hebrew manuscript by the hand of the scribe Shemu'el ben Ya'acob:

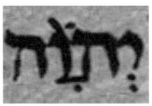

The name of our Heavenly Father written with
four consonants, three vowels, and an accent.

For anyone who wants to learn more about what this name means and how to pray, proclaim, praise, and pronounce it, *His Hallowed Name Revealed Again* is for you!

Enjoy the journey!

הֲלֹא מֵאָז הִשְׁמַעְתִּיךָ וְהִגַּדְתִּי

Have I not long since announced it to you and declared it?

ISAIAH 44:8

ב

BET

CHAPTER TWO

AN ANNOUNCEMENT FROM HEAVEN

Before there were any Scriptures, a long time ago, in a place far away, the Creator of the universe decided to reveal His word, including His name, in written form for all to see. I imagine an announcement was posted on a heavenly bulletin board that said, *All the host of heaven are invited to a meeting in the throne room at the time of the sighting of the new moon regarding the decision by the Holy Father to make His Holy Word available in written form. Please R.S.V.P. to Gabriel's office.*

Think of the buzz that would have been created among the angels if such an announcement was made. In their meeting one of the angels might have raised a hand, bowed his head, and asked our Heavenly Father something like, *"O Most High and Glorious, Omnipotent, Omniscient, and Omnipresent Creator of all that was, is and ever shall be, have You decided what the first recorded word from Your mouth will be?"* After a silence that perhaps seemed like an eternity, the answer would have come forth in words which sounded like thunder combined with rushing waters: *My first word spoken and recorded for all humankind to see will be based on My name. Yes, indeed! My holy name I will make known."*[8] I am convinced some angels would have begun cheering and clapping; some would have bowed down in worship; and others would have shouted, "Amen! Amen!" The angelic choir would have begun singing *Holy, Holy, Holy.* But wait a minute. What is your response?

Open your English Bible and look at this marvelous sight. In Genesis 1:3 the first four words out of the mouth of our Heavenly Father were, *"Let there be light."* Are you amazed? Are you moved to worship as I was? This English translation probably does not illicit the same response in you because it conceals the connection to the Hebrew name of our Heavenly Father, which is revealed in this verse and throughout the pages of Scripture. In the 1,574 pages of my Hebrew Bible the name יהוה appears 6,828 times.[9] This means that I can expect to find this holy name approximately four times on every page.

This same Hebrew name was taught to Moses while he was standing in front of a burning bush in the desert. Are you willing to be like Moses who slowed down, turned aside, and learned this holy name?

This same Hebrew name was introduced to millions of people at a mountain called Sinai, where our Heavenly Father spoke His name for all to hear. Open your English Bible and read it for yourself in Exodus 20:2. He says, "I am the LORD your God." Do you see it?

This same Hebrew name was read and spoken by *Jesus,* who, on a mountainside 2,000 years ago, taught the people to pray, "Our Father who art in heaven, hallowed be Thy name." Do you know that name?

This same Hebrew name that was introduced in heaven and taught on earth was placed in Jerusalem and is still there today! Do you believe it?

---

[8] Ezekiel 39:7.

[9] These are the four Hebrew letters (*yod hey vav hey*) that correspond to the English letters YHVH. They are the consonants of the personal name of the Creator of the universe that appear 6,828 times in the Hebrew manuscripts. Hebrew is written and read from right to left.

> In this house and in Jerusalem, which I have chosen from all the tribes of Israel, I will place My name forever.
>
> 2 KINGS 21:7

If you do believe that His name still dwells in Jerusalem, then you might also understand why I have felt His presence and continued to sing praises to His name ever since I first visited the ancient city called Zion.

> Sing praises to יהוה who dwells in Zion.
>
> PSALMS 9:11

A DISCOVERY ON EARTH

In 1979 an archeologist named Gabriel Barkay began an excavation of the tombs on the hill called Ketef Hinnom outside the walls of the Old City of Jerusalem. Because he was on a limited budget he used some 12- and 13-year-old children to be his "assistant archeologists."

> Among the thirteen-year-old diggers, there was one annoying kid named Nathan, who was always tugging at my shirt. I thought this was an ideal place to put him—he would be out of my sight. I told Nathan the repository had to be as clean as his mother's kitchen, even if he had to lick it. It had to be clean for the photography. Not too long afterwards, I felt him tugging at my shirt again. Nathan had in his hand almost complete pottery vessels. This time, I pulled at his shirt, took him back to the area and asked where he found them. Bored, Nathan had banged on the floor with a hammer. Under the rocks, he found the pottery.[10]

---

[10] http://www.itsgila.com/highlightspriestly.htm.

Young Nathan probably felt isolated while doing his mundane task of cleaning an old, dusty floor. He reportedly grew tired and bored with his job and began to do his own "digging." He was just banging on the floor, which finally gave way and uncovered a true treasure. This young Jewish boy, whose Hebrew name means *to give,* discovered the place where two small silver amulets were found. Inside these amulets were two silver scrolls.

These scrolls dated back to the time of the prophet Jeremiah before the destruction of the first temple around 500 B.C.E. The archeologists had an important decision to make. Should they go through the arduous and risky task of trying to unroll these two ancient witnesses to see what might be revealed? It took three years to create a technology that could unlock the treasure without causing irreversible damage to the contents of this amazing discovery.

These two scrolls revealed the oldest written biblical reference to the Hebrew name of our Heavenly Father. Wow! The biblical text written on these silver treasures was at least 400 years older than the earliest Dead Sea Scrolls, which were found by a young Arab boy in 1947. The Scripture reference is the blessing in Numbers 6:24-27. Within this blessing is the expectation of the pronunciation of the Hebrew name of our Heavenly Father. When His name is *set* (spoken) upon His people, the result is a blessing from Him.

The writing on the scrolls is in Paleo-Hebrew script.[11] This script was used by the Israelites before they were exiled to Babylon.

> The "Hebrew" alphabet, used in Modern Hebrew as well as in the Jewish Scriptures from the time of Ezra onward, is technically referred to as "Square Aramaic." This is because the Jewish scribes of the Babylonian Exile switched from the original alphabet of the Old Testament books, known to scholars as Paleo-Hebrew, to the Aramaic alphabet, because

---

[11] Paleo-Hebrew is derived from Hebrew letters have evolved over time.

Aramaic—"the Syrian tongue" of Ezra 4:7 (KJV)—
had by that time become the international language.[12]

Here is what His name looks like in this ancient Paleo-
Hebrew script (Ketef Hinnom font used by permission of Kris J.
Udd). I have also included the English translation of the passage:

𐤉𐤄𐤅𐤄 bless you and keep you,
𐤉𐤄𐤅𐤄 cause His face to shine upon you
𐤉𐤄𐤅𐤄 lift His face toward you and give you peace.
So they shall invoke[13] my name on the sons of Israel,
and I will bless them.

NUMBERS 6:24–27

Even though the letters look different, they represent the
same four-letter Hebrew name יהוה (YHVH) written on the front
cover and throughout this book. Young Nathan had to be willing to
dig and *tug* in order to give us this gift of the scroll with this
blessing-giving name. This book invites you to do the same.

In order to learn to proclaim this magnificent name, I had to
take the time to "unroll the scrolls" that hold the keys to
understanding it. I remember the choice I had to make when
Nehemia was explaining the issues surrounding the written
witnesses and the pronunciation of this Hebrew name:

> He explained a long series of linguistic and
> grammatical issues related to the pronunciation of
> the name. When he was done with this technical
> explanation he reminded me that there was still a
> great deal of valid debate about the true
> pronunciation of the name.[14]

---

[12] Associates for Biblical Research,
www.biblearchaeology.org/post/2010/01/06/The-Blessing-of-the-Silver-Scrolls.aspx.
[13] The Hebrew actually says וְשָׂמוּ אֶת שְׁמִי, which means "set" or "place" My name upon.
[14] N. Gordon and K. Johnson. *A Prayer to Our Father: Hebrew Origins of the Lord's Prayer.*
Hilkiah Press, 2009, pages 99-100.

We will *dig* and *tug* and venture into the deep waters of *"explanation"* in order to uncover the treasure of His name. The words *long, linguistic, grammatical, technical,* and *debate* sometimes scare people of faith because they want to keep things simple. My prayer is that I am able to present this information with integrity, as well as making it understandable for all who desire to praise and proclaim this magnificent and holy name.

The mere sight and mention of words and letters that look unfamiliar will cause discomfort for some readers. This is the audience I want to reach: people who have been conditioned to discount foreign things for fear that they may threaten or undermine their faith. Let's face this challenge head-on, believing that the desire for truth will ultimately overcome discouragement or fear. If you take your time and interact thoughtfully with this important information, it will become familiar and you will experience its life-changing effect.

> I wrote for them many thousands of things of My
> Torah,[15] but they regarded them as something alien.
> HOSEA 8:12

It is a sad truth that the teaching and instruction of the Torah are foreign to the present-day Christian Church. In fact, Hebrew, which is the original language of what Christians call the "Old Testament," is alien to many people of faith. Many readers will see the Hebrew letters placed throughout this book and feel they are looking at something too strange to comprehend. Unfortunately, some of them will put the book down and look for something more familiar. The most important Hebrew letters in this book are those that reveal the name of *Our Father who art in heaven.* It is this name that was read by kings, priests, prophets, and every biblical writer!

---

[15] Torah refers to the first five books of Moses. It is also a term used by many people to refer to the teaching and instruction in the entire "Old Testament."

We have been given various titles and substitutes, such as *Adonai, LORD,* and *God,* for our Heavenly Father's holy name. Those who should have conveyed this all-important name in the English translations have, for the most part, hidden it under layers of confusion and inconsistency. This holy name could have been expressed in our present-day language with ease. In fact, יהוה (YHVH)[16] made it so His name could flow out of our mouths with clarity, beauty, and power. Unfortunately, this name has practically been put under lock and key by those who consider us unqualified to handle it. This book gives access to the information and inspiration about this holy name so we can decide for ourselves if this name is for us.

BACK TO THE BASICS

As a result of spending the last several years studying the language, history, and culture of my Hebrew Bible, I now consider it to be my most prized possession. I spent well over 25 years in Christian ministry diligently studying my English Bible only to find out that I had merely scratched the surface. This includes the three years I studied for my Master of Divinity degree at Trinity Evangelical Seminary in Deerfield, Illinois. This does not mean that I wasted my time at Trinity Seminary. Quite the contrary. I was able to interact with some of the top biblical and theological scholars, past and present. I also consider my years at Trinity Seminary to have been some of the best years of my life. In fact, my seminary training prepared me to be able to reap the benefits of my present studies.

One of the ways that I was being prepared was through the study of both Greek and Hebrew. Unfortunately, my studies were based primarily on using these languages as tools for reference

---

[16] As stated earlier, יהוה is the Hebrew personal name of our Heavenly Father. The English rendering of these letters without the vowels is YHVH or YHWH. These four letters are commonly called the Tetragrammaton. As a reminder, Hebrew is written and read from right to left.

rather than really understanding their depth. Recently I have been able to dig further into Greek by comparing and contrasting the Hebrew and Greek versions of the Gospel of Matthew. This research was crucial in being able to gain a far deeper understanding of the Lord's Prayer in both Greek and Hebrew. I cannot imagine trying to do this without my language studies from seminary.

In order for me to really understand the name of our Heavenly Father, יהוה, I had to commit to immersing myself in my Hebrew Bible. What an absolute blessing it has been! It only made sense that if I wanted to understand how to call on His name, I needed to learn everything I could about the Hebrew language in which He revealed His name. This is when my search really became interesting. The more I studied about His name in the Hebrew manuscripts, the more questions I had about my English translation of the Bible. In order to get to the divine treasure, I had to be willing to sift through the layers of human agenda that were present in my English translation. If you are willing to do the same, you will not be disappointed.

I had to take a step back and look at the root of the problem. I have been encouraged by what I sense is a resurgence of Christians around the world who are examining their Hebrew heritage in the "Old Testament," which has so often been overlooked. The following statement makes the point well:

> But today we stand on the threshold of a new era. More and more Christians are coming to realize that Old Testament and Hebrew studies are not optional matters; indeed, they are the very bedrock upon which the Christian faith rests. They are what Paul refers to as "the holy Scriptures, which are able to make you wise for salvation" (2 Tim. 3:15). We must, therefore, continue urging a return to the position of the early Church, where today's Christian can, as John Bright has forcefully written, "claim the Old

Testament, as the New Testament did, for it belongs
to him no less than it did—and does—to Israel."[17]

I was a Christian who had conveniently disconnected myself
from my Hebrew roots and was trying to nourish myself on the
separate vine of modern-day Western Christianity. Once I realized
that I was "withering on the vine," I reconnected myself to the root
and the soil of my faith.

There are still countless Christians who haven't the slightest
awareness of their Hebrew heritage. I have gone into Christian
bookstores in various parts of the country looking for the blueprint
of our faith: the Hebrew Bible. I have asked many clerks and
managers if I could purchase one. More often than not, they've said
they have never seen a Hebrew Bible. I fear that the Christian
religion has become like an adopted child who denies his or her
family of origin. This must change. We must be willing to look into
the eyes of our Jewish brothers and sisters and see the resemblance.
We have the same Father!

Thorleif Boman writes the following in *Hebrew Thought
Compared with Greek:*

> Christianity arose on Jewish soil; Jesus and the
> Apostles spoke Aramaic, a language related to
> Hebrew, unless Harris Birkeland should prove to be
> right in his hypothesis that Jesus and the Apostles
> spoke a folk dialect of Hebrew. As the New
> Testament writings show, they were firmly rooted in
> the Old Testament and lived in its world of images.
> Shortly after the death of the Founder, however, the
> new religious community's centre of gravity shifted
> into the Greek-speaking Hellenistic world, and after
> the year 70, the community was severed finally from

---

[17] Wilson, Marvin. *Our Father Abraham: Jewish Roots of the Christian Faith.* Grand Rapids, Michigan, Wm. B. Eerdmans Publishing Company, 1989.

its motherland: Christianity has been the religion of Europeans ever since.[18]

I have had to take a serious look at my perceptions, which were shaped by a Greek mindset rather than a Hebrew mindset. I went to an evangelical school that taught that the manuscripts of the New Testament come from an inerrant Greek original text. I chose to take the six-week summer "suicide Greek" course in seminary because I wanted to learn as much Greek as I could so I could think like *Jesus* and the apostles. Well, it worked. I had become a full-fledged, Greek-thinking Christian. I have since realized that I was one-sided in my program of Greek immersion. Truthfully, Western Christianity is also one-sided when it comes to Greek and Hebrew. I call this the right-hand vs. the left-hand struggle.

I have a friend named Chet who works at the local UPS store. Whenever I go there to send a package, Chet usually asks a question or two about something I've written on the shipping form. I really dislike the tiny forms and the cheap, leaky pens. One day Chet said something that had a profound effect on me. He admitted that he, too, had bad penmanship (who said I had bad penmanship?), but this was because from an early age he was forced to write with the wrong hand. You see, Chet's parents believed in the age-old superstition that the left hand is cursed. So whenever they saw their son using his left hand, they slapped it. Chet caught on quickly and learned to do most things, including writing, with his right hand. Eventually he became so accustomed to using his right hand that he even forgot he had been born left-handed. Throughout his school years Chet struggled with sloppy handwriting until one day, in a moment of compassion, his father suggested, "Why don't you try your left hand?" Unfortunately, by then it was too late for Chet to re-learn how to write with his left hand.

---

[18] Boman, Thorleif. *Hebrew Thought Compared with Greek.* New York: W. W. Norton, 1960. page 17.

Beginning in the second century, Christianity underwent its own hand-slapping campaign. The main focus of this process was the eradication of anything that was too "left-handed" in its orientation. Although *Jesus* and all his original disciples were Jewish, the Church labeled the Jews as accursed in the eyes of the Christian God. Anything that was deemed too Jewish was expunged from the Christian faith. Some people involved in the early formation of the Church followed this to its logical conclusion, proclaiming the God of the Old Testament to be separate and distinct from the Christian God of the New Testament. By the fourth century, the hand slapping by the Church led to the violent persecution of the Jewish descendants of the original followers of *Jesus,* who were deemed heretics for continuing to observe the ancient rites and rituals of the Old Testament.

I am concerned that the Church has moved so far from the foundations of our faith that we have forgotten our left-handed origins. It is impossible to understand what the one who is called *Jesus* taught us if we don't understand and appreciate the Jewish culture and Hebrew language in which he lived and preached. Even the famous Protestant Reformer Martin Luther once said:

> The Hebrew language is the best language of all. . . . If I were younger I would want to learn this language, because no one can really understand the Scriptures without it. For, although the New Testament is written in Greek, it is full of Hebraisms and Hebrew expressions. It has therefore been aptly said that the Hebrews drink from the spring, the Greeks from the stream that flows from it, and the Latins from a downstream puddle.[19]

I wonder what image Martin Luther would give for present-day Christians who have been limited to the confines of the English

---

[19] Translation adapted from P. Lapide, *Hebrew in the Church,* translated by E. F. Rhodes, Grand Rapids, 1984, page x.

translation of their Bible. Maybe they drink from the bottled water that English translators gathered up from the puddle. Who knows?

Without this appreciation of what we might call the left-handed origins of our faith, the Church is losing the understanding of who our Creator is according to His word and who we are called to be according to His will. Rather than returning to an understanding of Scripture in its original linguistic and historical context, our present-day Church is moving into the feel-good, nature-focused, undefined, unclear, unexplainable *"what have you done for me lately"* god who changes colors like the horses of the Emerald City in the movie *The Wizard of Oz.* He is the green god for those who believe in prosperity theology, the black god for those who adhere to liberation theology, the white god for racists, the black-and-white god for the reconciliation movement, the red, white, and blue god for the conservatives, and the rainbow-colored god for the liberals. Such groups have attempted to limit the Omnipotent, Omnipresent, and Omniscient Almighty Creator of heaven and earth. These and other -ologies, -isms and -tions are desperately looking for ways to control people and contain God.

A number of years ago I was encouraged by my Heavenly Father to "try my left hand." I decided to go through the sometimes difficult and always humbling process of learning to be proficient with my left-handed origins. At times I feel the heat from the flames of criticism when I choose not to bow down to the noise of the religious control-mongers who insist that I stop using my left hand. Shadrach, Meshach, and Abednego provide a biblical model for standing up for conviction rather than bowing down to religious control. Other times I want to complain like Moses that *"I am slow of speech"* regarding the Hebrew language. However, I keep hearing the voice of יהוה encouraging me that *"He made my mouth, and that He is with me."*

When some people hear that I have co-authored a book with a Jewish friend about the Hebrew origins of the Lord's

Prayer,[20] they want to slap my hand. Because of their desire to control people and their attempt to contain the uncontainable One, they are fearful of people like me. So no matter how hard they slap my hand, I won't be trained like Chet. I won't let them force me away from the left-handed history, culture, and language of my prized possession: the Hebrew Holy Scriptures.

It is a tragic truth that many of those so-called "Church Fathers" were master hand-slappers, and as a result of their words, theologies, and actions, they have trained Christians over the last 2,000 years to be suspicious of *the Jews* and anything too "left-handed." I would encourage you to check the many disappointing and disparaging statements of individuals such as Ignatius, Bishop of Antioch (98-117), Justin Martyr (138-161), Origen of Alexandria (185-254), John Chrysostom (344-407), St. Augustine (354-430), John Calvin (1509-1564) and, as I already mentioned, Martin Luther. I just could not bring myself to quote some of the critical and negative statements that these and other founders of Christianity have made against my Jewish brothers and sisters. I encourage you to do your own research on the anti-Semitism of the Christian Church Fathers and those who followed in their steps.

Rather than allowing the voices of history to condition my mind, I have learned to let the Holy Scriptures, according to their historical, cultural, and linguistic context, define our Heavenly Father. He cannot be defined by our modern social, economic, racial, religious, or gender biases. I encourage all of those who are not willing to be controlled and are not afraid to have their hands slapped while on this journey, to extend the right hand of fellowship and reach out to our original family of faith. I also challenge you to "try your left hand" and grasp the deep revelations that come from the original Hebrew language of Scripture.

By both extending my right hand of fellowship to my Jewish brothers and sisters and grasping the Hebrew Holy Words of our Heavenly Father with my left hand, my study life has gone to a level

---

[20] N. Gordon and K. Johnson. *A Prayer to Our Father: Hebrew Origins of the Lord's Prayer*, Hilkiah Press, 2009.

I could not have imagined. As a result, I have been blessed beyond measure and deeply motivated to share what I have learned about *His hallowed name.*

I invite you to come on a journey with me as the Hebrew manuscripts reveal the name that will ultimately be the one name you will need to know!

> In that day יהוה will be king over all the earth; in that day יהוה will be one and His name one.
>
> ZECHARIAH 14:9

This will be an exciting and revealing journey through Scripture. I recommend that you read every footnote and every passage referenced. May our Heavenly Father speak to your heart through the pages of Scripture and this book so you can grasp the depth and riches of His holy name יהוה.

> And on that day the deaf shall hear the words of a book, and out of their gloom and darkness the eyes of the blind shall see. . . . But when he [Jacob] sees his children, the work of My hands in his midst, they will sanctify My name. . . .
>
> ISAIAH 29:18, 23

There are people who are looking, listening, and waiting for the day when the truth about this awesome name will burst forth and find its place in their hearts. These are the people who are ready for *His Hallowed Name Revealed Again.*

This book is your invitation to a meeting where you will learn to understand, pray, proclaim, pronounce, see, sing, and sanctify the name of our Heavenly Father, יהוה. Are you willing to R.S.V.P.?

נִבְחָר שֵׁם מֵעֹשֶׁר רָב

A good name is to be desired more than great wealth.

PROVERBS 22:1

ג

GIMEL

CHAPTER THREE

THE INGREDIENTS IN A NAME

Giving your children names they will appreciate throughout life is a daunting task. Anyone who knows me well will confirm that I have never liked my name. As long as I can remember there has been a story in my family that goes like this. My mother planned to give me the name Kevin. My aunt heard my future name and decided she would name her son Kevin. Since my cousin was born first, he got the name. My parents had already decided that all their children would have names beginning with *K,* so Keith, from a Gaelic word meaning "forest," was their last-minute choice. Both the story and the name—so dull to my ear—will forever disappoint me. In our Western culture there is not the same appreciation for name giving and receiving as there is in the Hebrew culture.

People often name their children based on how the name sounds or what is popular, and not for what it means. This was clearly the case with my parents' decision about my boring name. Not so in Hebrew culture. As Marvin Wilson writes:

> In Hebrew thought, the name of an individual was considered to be more than a title or a label for

identification. Rather, a name was believed to reveal the essence, character, reputation, or destiny of the one to whom it was given. This is why the moral law of Moses forbids defamation of another's name by false witness (Exod. 20:16). Indeed, "a good name [i.e., reputation] is more desirable than great riches" (Prov. 22:1). Thus the name of every Hebrew sent out some sort of message with it.[21]

When we look at the Scriptures we find many references to the giving and receiving of names. The idea of names comes from the Creator Himself. Therefore, we should expect that when He gives a name, there is always a meaning behind it. Certainly this is true in the case of His name and the many beautiful and powerful descriptions of Him throughout the Hebrew text.

As I was conducting research for this book, I made an interesting discovery. In our English Bibles the word *GOD* is at times inserted in place of the Hebrew name יהוה rather than using the other popular English title LORD. But neither of these English titles can compare to our Heavenly Father's actual name. The reason I found this interesting is because the word *GOD* has no linguistic connection with the Hebrew name יהוה, yet the English translators freely used it to replace His holy name. I needed some clarity about this English word *God*.

I have read about the pagan roots of many words, including *God*.[22] This investigation led me to Webster's Dictionary to see how it describes the word *God*. I expected to see two entries, one for *God* (capital *G*) and one for *god* (small *g*). I know there is a clear distinction made in Scripture between the foreign and false gods and the *God* of creation. Surely Webster would give honor to the

[21] Wilson, Marvin. *Our Father Abraham: Jewish Roots of the Christian Faith*. Grand Rapids, Michigan, Wm. B. Eerdmans Publishing Company, 1989, pages 180–81.
[22] C. J. Koster. *Come Out of Her, My People*, Institute for Scripture Research Ltd.; 5th edition (January 1, 2004), pages 53–57.

"big *G*." What I found convicted me and motivated me to make an author's decision. How do you feel about the following definition?

> god \ gäd *also* god\ *n* [ME, fr. OE; akin to OHG *got* god] **1** *cap* : the supreme being or ultimate reality: as **a** : the Being perfect in power, wisdom, and goodness whom men worship as creator and ruler of the universe **b** *Christian Science* : the incorporeal divine Principle ruling over all as eternal Spirit : infinite Mind **2** : a being or object believed to have more than natural attributes and powers and to require man's worship; *specif* : one controlling a particular aspect or part of reality **3** : a person or thing of supreme value **4** : a powerful ruler

This definition disappointed me. Webster could have at least given a separate entry and a longer, more appropriate definition of "the supreme or ultimate reality." I realize that *God* is the accepted word in our English language and is even printed on our money. However, I have decided that in this book I will focus on many of our Heavenly Father's wonderful descriptions and names that are evident throughout the Hebrew Scriptures.

Because I wish to give the reader a glimpse behind the English version of our Bible into these Hebrew jewels, I have decided to do an experiment. In the popular King James Version of the Bible the word *God* is used 2,667 times, translated from the four Hebrew words אל (El), אלה (Elah), אלוה (Eloah), and אלהים (Elohim).[23] Every time I normally would use *God* in this book I will instead insert one of the Hebrew descriptions or names of the Creator. I will make an exception when quoting Scripture; then I will use the actual Hebrew word that appears in the text (El, Elah, Eloah, or Elohim) in place of the English word *God*. As I am sure you have already noticed, I have substituted the four Hebrew

---

[23] These three Hebrew words and the Aramaic word *Elah* are translated into English as "God" or "god."

letters יהוה in place of the title LORD in Scripture references. One benefit of this exercise is that you can actually learn to read and speak a little biblical Hebrew.

If I run out of Hebrew titles or names without repeating one before ending this book, then I will revert back to using the English title *God*. I just think that since these beautiful and powerful Hebrew descriptions and titles are available, why not share them with you? In light of the subject matter of this book, I just cannot bring myself to use this very popular and common English substitute for the Omnipotent, Omniscient, and Omnipresent Supreme Ruler; Sustainer; Merciful, Loving, Most High, Eternal Creator; and Savior of the Universe. He is worthy to receive glory, honor, and praise from our mouths and our dictionaries.

By way of clarification, I am *not* saying that if a person uses the word *God* that he or she is in error. I just want to take the opportunity to bring people into contact with the *biblical words* that describe our Heavenly Father.

Let's begin this exercise of "trying our left hand" by learning some of the Hebrew descriptions of אלהים (Mighty One).[24] From this point forward I will place the Hebrew word, followed by the English meaning of the description in parenthesis. I will also place the pronunciation and Scripture reference in the footnotes. Since the words of the Hebrew Bible are available, and can be easily spoken, it will be an honor to use those words in this book.

There is an English translation of the Bible called *The Scriptures* that uses the original Hebrew words for the word *God* when referring to this particular title. The following statement gives the rationale for this translation decision:

> At this stage we need to explain the Hebrew word "Elohim" used in this translation. English translations have traditionally rendered it as "God" or as "god(s)" in most instances. However the Hebrew word "elohim" is the plural form of "eloah,"

---

[24] Elohim, Genesis 1:1.

which has the basic meaning of "mighty one." This word is not only used for deity, but is used in Scripture for judges, angels and idols (Shemoth / Ex. 7:1; 9:28; 12:12; 22:8, 9; Tehillim / Ps. 8:5; 82:1, 6) besides being used frequently for the Almighty. The shorter forms, "el" and "elim" have the same basic meaning and similar usage. (Needless to say, the same applies to the Aramaic equivalents, such as "elah" and "elahin.") By transliterating these expressions instead of translating them as "Mighty One" we discovered a richness in them, and therefore retained them, with the exception of a few instances (noted in footnotes), where the translation of "mighty one" or "mighty ones" seemed more appropriate.[25]

It is important to mention here that some Jewish people are uncomfortable using the Hebrew word *Elohim* for God. In fact, many Orthodox Jews will actually add a "k" sound for the "h" so that they say *"Elokim"* rather than *"Elohim"* when referring to *God.* Some will also write *G-d* rather than *God* when referring to Elohim in print. As you go through this book you will understand their reasons for these practices. In fact, they come from the same tradition as the one that alters both the writing and pronunciation of יהוה, the name of our Heavenly Father. I will discuss this in detail later.

I hope you can make the transition from English titles to Hebrew descriptions without too much frustration or discomfort. This exercise can ultimately prepare you to know how to write and pronounce the Holy Name that goes beyond titles and descriptions to the very character and nature of our Heavenly Father. I am fully aware of the mental gymnastics you will go through when you see these "backwards and ancient" letters on the page. However, studies suggest that the average human only uses a small percentage

[25] *The Scriptures.* Northriding, South Africa: Institute for Scripture Research, 2002. p. xiii.

of his mental capacity. Why not take advantage of our dormant brain capacity to tap into the power of His name? I am confident that He will open the mind of the willing as He did for me. Just call on the One who will give you this confidence. He is called יהוה מבטחי (יהוה my confidence).[26]

Now back to the subject of the ingredients in a Hebrew name. There is a wonderful picture of אל חי (Living El)[27] as the ultimate life- and name-giver who also delegated this job of naming to His people. As early as Genesis 2:19 we find that Adam, the first man, was given his first job as the namer of animals. What a miracle! Adam was able to come up with creative names for how many species? By the time we get to Genesis 2:23, Adam moved from naming animals to being the first person to give a name to another person: his wife. With this in mind, let's take a look at the earliest record of name-giving to see if we can learn anything about the first two people created: Adam and Eve.

The first time the word *Adam* is mentioned is in Genesis 1:26. The following verse is my attempt at translation in what I call the KJV—"Keith Johnson Version." Before you get nervous, I am not claiming my own version of the Bible. I am simply giving you a little Hebrew background to compare with your favorite translation. It just so happens that my "boring name" has the same initials as the popular King James Version. As I mentioned at the beginning of this book, it will be helpful to have at least two other Bible versions to compare against my version.

> Then Elohim said, "Let us make Adam in our image. . . ."
>
> GENESIS 1:26

Obviously, this is not how most English Bibles render this verse. However, the Hebrew word for man in this verse is אדם (Adam). Please note that Hebrew is read from right to left. The

---

[26] יהוה Mivtachee, Psalms 71:5.
[27] El Chai, Joshua 3:10.

word *Adam* can be translated as man or humankind. There are biblical examples of both. The following verse is speaking about humankind, not the man Adam:

> He created them male and female and He called their name Adam.
>
> GENESIS 5:2

This is what we can see on the surface. Hebrew is a beautiful language that is phonetic, numeric, and pictorial. In other words, every Hebrew letter has a sound, a number, and a picture. Extensive study of the language has shown that Hebrew was originally written with pictures. I encourage you to research what the letters looked like. These pictures still exist today for every Hebrew letter. It is amazing how revealing they can be with the accompanying Hebrew words.

Before we move on, I need to offer a word of caution and some background on Hebrew word-pictures. Unfortunately, there are people who take this aspect of the Hebrew language to an extreme, not unlike the study of numerology in kabbalistic teachings. True Hebrew word-pictures do not *create* theology; they only, at times, paint an informative picture that I find intriguing. Hebrew word-pictures are a fascinating study that can enhance our understanding of the language. I have found many sources of information on this subject, both old and new. There are simple books such as *Hebrew Word Pictures,* by Dr. Frank T. Seekins, and classic scholarly sources such as *Gesenius' Hebrew Grammar,* edited by E. Kautzsch and A.E. Cowley. I was also able to do some research on ancient word-pictures at the Israel National Museum. Let's take a quick look at some of the creative ways word-pictures can be interpreted.

We can begin with the first human being, who was named Adam. The first letter of Adam's name is א (*aleph*). This is equivalent to the English letter *a.* The word-picture associated with this letter is an ox head, so one meaning that the א (*aleph*) can convey is "strength, leader, or first."

The next two letters of Adam are ד (*dalet*) and ם (*mem*). The ד (*dalet*) pictures a door or path. The ם (*mem*) word-picture is water. One possible meaning of just these two letters could be "the path of water." Guess which Hebrew word these two letters spell? The letters דם spell the Hebrew word for *blood*. What carries water and oxygen through our bodies? Blood! The name אדם (*Adam*) can be seen as the word-picture "first blood." Adam was the "first man" created. Also, you may not know that the English word translated as ground is אדמה (*adamah*). This is the feminine form of the word *Adam*. From what did the Creator form Adam? *Adamah* or ground.[28] The feminine ground (*adamah*) brought forth the first man Adam. Maybe that is why we speak of "Mother Earth."

The first woman created was named Eve. Notice, however, that she was not initially given this name. Rather, she was "called" woman.[29] There is an interesting play on the Hebrew words for *woman* and *man*. When אל אחד בראנו (One El created us)[30] brought the woman to Adam, he said, *"This at last is bone of my bones and flesh of my flesh and she shall be called אשה [ishah]."* This Hebrew word is translated as woman. Then Adam explains why she is called אשה (*ishah*). He says, *"Because she was taken out of man."* He uses the word איש (*ish*), which is another word for *man*. In Hebrew it reads like this: "She shall be called אשה [ishah] because she was taken out of איש [ish]." Notice that the next time the word איש (*ish*) is used is when Eve refers to her son Cain. She says, "I have gotten an איש [ish, man]."[31] She did not use the word *adam* as man, but rather the same root word that Adam used for her when she was first named, אשה (*ishah*). These are known as "word puns" (plays on words). They occur countless times throughout the Hebrew Scriptures.

Eventually Adam sinned and was "called into account" by אל קנא (Jealous El)[32] who desired to have intimate fellowship with

---

[28] Genesis 2:7.
[29] Genesis 2:23.
[30] El Ehad Bera'anu, Malachi 2:10.
[31] Genesis 4:1.
[32] El Kanna, Exodus 20:5.

the couple in the garden. Adam then gave the woman a new name. Scripture says that he called his wife's name Eve חוה (*chavah*, Genesis 3:20). Again, the meaning of her name is explained: "Because she was the mother of all living." Notice two words, *mother* and *living*. Mother is the Hebrew word אם (*em*), and living is חי (*chai*). The word-picture for mother starts out like Adam. One possible interpretation of this word-picture is that the א is the "strength, leader, or first." The מ (*mem*) corresponds to the English letter *m*. The word-picture for מ (*mem*) is water. The mother is the "strong water." Mothers bring forth life חי (*chai*) through birth water that leads the child out. As you can see, it takes a healthy imagination to do this exercise. That is why word-picture analysis is not meant to *create* theology or to be considered an exact science. I certainly would be suspicious of any attempt to dramatically extract theological messages from word-pictures.

There are numerous examples of our Heavenly Father and His children giving names to people, places, and things. In all of the giving and receiving of names something interesting happens that we can only understand by having a little knowledge of Hebrew. The English Bible cannot do justice to this significant theme in Scripture.

Take a journey with me regarding the significance of the word *name* (*shem*). Noah was 500 years old and he became the father of Shem, Ham, and Japheth. These three sons became the fathers of many nations. In Genesis 10 it says:

> These are the generations of Shem, Ham, and Japheth, the sons of Noah; and sons were born to them after the flood.
>
> GENESIS 10:1

> These are the sons of Shem, according to their families, according to their languages, by their lands, according to their nations.
>
> GENESIS 10:31

Do you understand the significance of the name given to Noah's first son? The name *Shem* is the Hebrew word שֵׁם (*shem*), which means *name*. This may seem inconsequential at this point; however, there is an important connection between the man named Shem and the following passage, where something very subtle happens. The Scripture says:

> And they said, "Come let us build for ourselves a city, and a tower whose top will reach into heaven, and make for ourselves a name[שֵׁם, *shem*], otherwise we will be scattered abroad over the face of the whole earth."
>
> GENESIS 11:4

What is the connection between Shem, the son of Noah, and the men making a name (*shem*) for themselves? Try translating the above verse this way: "And let us make for ourselves a *shem* [name]." It is this statement that causes the name-giver יהוה to come down to see what is going on. Now take special note of this verse:

> These are the generations of Shem [name].
>
> GENESIS 11:10

Guess who comes from the blood line of Shem? Abram. Notice what יהוה, the name-giver and covenant-keeper, says when he enters Abram's life.

> And I will make you a great nation, and I will bless you, and make your *shem* [name] great; and so you shall be a blessing.
>
> GENESIS 12:2

It is from the lineage of Shem (name) that the name-giver, יהוה, will make another man's name (*shem*) great. But before that happens, Noah's descendants try to make their own *shem* (name) great. This seems to be what is happening in the world today. Many people are interested in making a great *shem* (name) for themselves, while ignoring the name-maker who has a name He wants to give them. This is the first of many themes in Scripture that show just how important the issue of "name" (שֵׁם *shem*) is to יהוה.

So what about His name? By now I hope you realize that the four Hebrew letters that you have been seeing are the building blocks to understanding the name יהוה. Many modern-day Jews often refer to יהוה as *Hashem,* which literally means "the name." But is that as far as these four letters go in terms of meaning? Absolutely not! These four letters are the keys to getting to the very essence of אל דעות (El of Knowledge).[33] In a way, they are like the four chemical letters *A, T, G,* and *C* that make up our DNA (deoxyribonucleic acid).

When James Watson and Francis Crick discovered the structure of DNA in 1953, they literally unveiled its power as well as its beauty. In many scientists' minds this discovery was like uncovering "the secret of life." If you could uncoil a single strand of DNA it would reach six feet in length. If you were to place each of the trillions of strands that are in your body from end to end, they would span the width and breadth of our solar system. If you fold one strand back up, it would shrink to only a few trillionths of an inch, small enough to fit in any one of the seventy-five to one hundred trillion cells that comprise each human body. DNA carries the recipe for making a human being from scratch.

Similar to Watson and Crick, you now have an opportunity to make an even more amazing discovery. The beauty and power of the name of the Almighty Creator of the universe is within the four letters יהוה (*yod hey vav hey*). These four letters of the name of our Heavenly Father will bring you to the depth of the riches of the nature and character of אל גדול ונורא (El Great and Awesome).[34]

There are two more passages that I need to share to help set the context for this important topic of the name יהוה. The first is in

---

[33] El De'oat, 1 Samuel 2:3.
[34] El Gadol Venorah, Deuteronomy 7:21.

Genesis 32 where Jacob (soon to be named Israel) was in a wrestling match with אל הנראה (El Who Appeared).[35] In the midst of the struggle Jacob asked to be blessed before he would let go. So יהוה asked,

> "What is your name?" . . . He said, "Your name shall no longer be Jacob, but Israel; for you have striven with Elohim and with men and have prevailed."
>
> GENESIS 32:27–28

This amazing verse gives us some insight into the importance of the meaning behind a Hebrew name. Jacob asked for a blessing, so יהוה changed his name to Israel. When יהוה changed Jacob's name, he was letting both Jacob and us know what was coming. In fact, I think the Canaanites, Jebusites, Amorites, Hivites, Hittites, and every other group that considered themselves enemies of Israel, would have done well to understand the blessing of Jacob's change of name. Because of this name change Israel was, and still is, well-equipped for a wrestling match.

This is why it is more important for us to listen to the Scriptures than to the news. We should not be surprised when we hear that there are wrestling matches among the descendants of Jacob. We should also expect Israel's seed to prevail. This is not wishful thinking, rather it is realizing the power of a name given by יהוה. Israel has both struggle and victory built into its name!

After Jacob prevailed he made another request. He wanted to know the name of the One who could change a name, so he asked,

> "Please tell me your name." But he said, "Why is it that you ask my name?" And he blessed him there.
>
> GENESIS 32:29

---

[35] El Hanear'eh, Genesis 35:1.

34

For some reason, אל בית אל (El of the House of El)[36] chose not to explain anything about His name in the place where He revealed His presence. It is clear that Jacob already knew the name יהוה because he proclaimed it several times.[37] This might be one of the explanations for the statement יהוה made to Moses:

> I am יהוה; and I appeared to Abraham, Isaac, and Jacob, as El Shaddai,[38] but by My name, יהוה, I did not make Myself known to them.
>
> EXODUS 6:2-3

Our Heavenly Father, יהוה, apparently did not make known the full essence of His name to anyone before Moses. Notice that He connects appearing with making His name known. Even though Abraham, Isaac and Jacob all knew the name יהוה, there was something more about its meaning that had not yet been revealed.[39] I will address this issue in more detail in Chapter Ten.

It is also interesting that in the book of Judges there is another interaction with someone who asked about our Heavenly Father's name. Manoah asked the angel of יהוה,

> "What is your name . . . ?" But the angel of יהוה said to him, "Why do you ask my name, seeing that it is wonderful?"
>
> JUDGES 13:17–18

Let me offer a quick Hebrew lesson. The English word *wonderful* is translated from the Hebrew word פלאי, which is pronounced "peli." There are only two times in the entire Hebrew Scriptures where this exact form of this Hebrew word is used. The first time is in Judges and the other is in the Psalms:

[36] El Bet El, Genesis 35:7.
[37] Genesis 27:20; 28:13, 16, 20-21.
[38] El Almighty, literally means El of my breasts, Exodus 6:3.
[39] For more on these verses see Genesis 14:19-20 and the next chapter under the section about the Most High.

You have enclosed me behind and before, and laid Your hand upon me. Such knowledge is too wonderful [פלאי *peli*] for me; it is too high, I cannot attain to it.

PSALMS 139:5–6

It is amazing that האל עשה פלא (The El Who Works Wonders) [40] reserved this word of wonder פלאי (*peli*) for His name and His knowledge. He chooses who, when, where, why, and how to reveal His name. How remarkable it is that we have been chosen to know our Heavenly Father יהוה by His *wonderful* name! Are you still with me? If so, let's continue this wondrous journey!

---

[40] Ha El Osay Phele, Psalms 77:14 in English and 77:15 in the Hebrew Scriptures.

כִּי הִגְדַּלְתָּ עַל כָּל שִׁמְךָ אִמְרָתֶךָ

For You have exalted above everything, Your name and Your word.

PSALMS 138:2 (Keith Johnson Version)

ד

DALET

CHAPTER FOUR

ABOVE EVERYTHING

Does the name יהוה matter to you? Maybe you are asking what is so important about knowing the personal name of our Heavenly Father when we have the perfectly good and acceptable English title LORD? If Psalms 138:2 quoted above is correct, and I hope you will check for yourself, it means that there is nothing that the Father exalts above His name and His word. The English title LORD is not His name; it is merely a word used by man to conceal the name that this book will help you know and understand.

There is a unique interaction between Moses and יהוה that illustrates the importance of this name. Moses makes an interesting request. He says, "I pray You, show me Your glory!"[41] and יהוה responds by saying,

> I Myself will make all My goodness pass before you,
> and will proclaim the name יהוה before you; and I

---

[41] Exodus 33:18.

will be gracious to whom I will be gracious, and will show compassion on whom I will show compassion.

EXODUS 33:19

Notice that the request is answered by the promise of His presence and the proclamation of His name. Not only does יהוה promise to proclaim His name, He also explains it with beauty and power. What a wonderful combination of His name followed by grace and compassion. The Scripture says that after Moses cut the two tablets of stone like the former ones, יהוה wrote the words on the new tablets. Can you imagine the hand of אל רחום וחנון (El Compassionate and Gracious)[42] writing His teaching and instruction on stone tablets? This is a picture of what He wants to do with His people. Our compassionate and gracious El wants to write His Torah on our hearts.[43]

When יהוה descended to show Moses His glory, He did something very revealing:

> יהוה descended in the cloud and stood with him there and proclaimed the name יהוה. יהוה passed before him and proclaimed, "יהוה יהוה El, compassionate and gracious, slow to anger, and abounding in steadfast love and faithfulness."

EXODUS 34:5–6 (Keith Johnson Version)

Twice יהוה proclaims His name in front of Moses. We will see as we continue this journey that there is something special about the number *two*. One of my "quirks" is that I love numbers. You will notice that the number *two* appears frequently in this book. I understand it to be a number that represents valid testimony.[44] When something has at least *two* witnesses it catches my attention and stirs my imagination. Could it be that יהוה was

---

[42] El Rachum Vechanun, Exodus 34:6.
[43] Jeremiah 31:33.
[44] Deuteronomy 17:6.

proclaiming His name as a witness for both heaven and earth? While you decide on the theological or biblical validity of my little quirk, allow me to *italicize* the significant *twos* that occur on our journey of discovery.

After making the *two* declarations of His name, יהוה goes on to proclaim and explain even further just what this name is about. He proclaims patience, abounding love, and truth. I want to know this name that delivers these characteristics. Moses asks for יהוה to show His glory, so what does He do? He proclaims His name! How important is the personal name יהוה? So important that אל הכבוד (El of Glory)[45] makes a direct connection between His glory and His name! This must be why the psalmist says:

> Ascribe to יהוה the glory due to His name. . . .
> PSALMS 29:2

The Most High

In Genesis 14 we find the story of King Melchizedek of Salem, whom the Scripture says was priest of אל עליון (El Most High)[46]. He blesses Abram by saying,

> Blessed be Abram by El Elyon, maker of heaven and earth. And blessed be El Elyon who has delivered your enemies into your hand.
> GENESIS 14:19–20

Afterward, when Abram addresses the King of Sodom, he uses the same title but includes the name יהוה before it. He says, *"I have sworn to יהוה El Elyon, maker of heaven and earth . . ."* (verse 22). The priest uses only the title; Abram proclaims His name.

---

[45] El Hakavode, Psalms 29:3.
[46] El Elyon, Genesis 14:18.

Are you convinced of how important this *sanctified* name is to our Heavenly Father? I hope so because our prophetic future is tied to knowing the name יהוה.

> But you, O יהוה, abide forever; and Your name to all generations. You will arise and have compassion on Zion; for it is time to be gracious to her, for the appointed time has come. Surely Your servants find pleasure in her stones and feel pity for her dust. So the nations will fear the name יהוה and all the kings of the earth Your glory. For יהוה has built up Zion; He has appeared in His glory. He has regarded the prayer of the destitute and has not despised their prayer. This will be written for the generation to come, that a people yet to be created may praise י׳. For He looked down from His holy height; from heaven יהוה gazed upon the earth, to hear the groaning of the prisoner, to set free those who were doomed to death, that men may tell of the name יהוה in Zion and his praise in Jerusalem; when the peoples are gathered together, and the kingdoms, to serve יהוה.
>
> PSALMS 102:12–22

In the passage above the personal name of אלי מלכי (My El, My King)[47] is mentioned seven times! He is the One who will rule His kingdom forever. The nations who do not know His name now will definitely know it then!

> My holy name I will make known in the midst of My people Israel; and I will not let My holy name be profaned anymore. And the nations will know that I am יהוה, the Holy One in Israel.
>
> EZEKIEL 39:7

---

[47] Eli Malki (the ending of both words sound like key), Psalms 68:24. Did you notice that one time His name is spelled differently in Psalms 102? Keep reading!

"For from the rising of the sun even to its setting, My name will be great among the nations, and in every place incense is going to be offered to My name, and a grain offering that is pure; for My name will be great among the nations," says יהוה of hosts.

MALACHI 1:11

One of my favorite passages in all of Scripture reminds us that יהוה desires to respond to His people who are called by His name:

And [if] My people who are called by My name humble themselves and pray and seek My face and turn from their wicked ways, then I will hear from heaven, will forgive their sin and will heal their land.

2 CHRONICLES 7:14

If nothing until now has convinced you of the importance of the name יהוה, maybe this will. His name is our help! At the very moment I was writing this line I received what I consider one of those phone calls that came right on time, a fulfillment of the promise of His name יהוה עזרנו (יהוה Our Help).[48] That phone call truly helped me during a time of struggle! I have learned to wait and hope in the One who helps me. Do you need any help? Call on His name!

Our soul waits for יהוה; He is our help and our shield.

PSALMS 33:20

Our help is in the name יהוה, who made heaven and earth.

PSALMS 124:8

---

48 יהוה Azrenu, Psalms 33:20.

The exalted name יהוה can open our eyes, raise our heads, show us love, protect strangers, support the fatherless and widows, while at the same time thwarting the way of the wicked! How about that for a name?

> יהוה opens the eyes of the blind; יהוה raises up those who are bowed down; יהוה loves the righteous; יהוה protects the strangers; He supports the fatherless and the widow, but He thwarts the way of the wicked.
>
> PSALMS 146:8–9

In order to reap the benefits of reading this book, you must be willing to take a position of humility so you can receive the blessing, forgiveness, and help that come from being called by the name יהוה, which is exalted above everything! You also must balance that humility with the desire to experience the power of His name. Are you ready? Are you willing?

Power-Packed Name

In the fall of 2002, after my trip to Jerusalem, I was traveling with my oldest son, Taylor, to visit a college and see friends. While I was on the airplane, I heard what seemed like a familiar voice say, "The time has come to write the book." As I was sharing what I had just heard with my son, flight attendants rushed down the aisle with oxygen tanks. My son and I, along with many other passengers, were confused and, I must confess, a little concerned; okay, scared. I looked behind me and saw a man in military uniform two rows back looking very flushed. There was an announcement from the flight attendant that said, "Ladies and gentlemen, we have a problem with one of our passengers. When we land we are asking you to stay seated as the paramedics come on board." As we were preparing to land, the flight attendants were trying to administer oxygen to this young soldier. When we finally arrived at the gate, the paramedics boarded and administered their care.

When we were eventually allowed off the plane, I saw a picture of what was, for me, my first call to write what I knew at the time about the name יהוה. That man seemed to symbolize the many people who are suffering from a lack of biblical revelation. The paramedics represented "the truth" that must come aboard in order to revive the people. I am convinced that as we come to a place of accepting that יהוה has revealed His name *again,* we will have the fresh oxygen of knowledge, revelation, and truth to be the people that אל אמת (El of Truth)[49] has called us to be in this world. We will no longer suffer a lack of oxygen because of the desires and traditions of man. I fear that if the oxygen of knowledge, truth, and revelation is not administered by the churches and synagogues, then judgment will fall from אל גמלות (El of Recompense/Deeds).[50]

> My people are destroyed for lack of knowledge. Because you have rejected knowledge, I also will reject you from being my priest. . . .
>
> HOSEA 4:6

There is a statement in the book of Exodus that sets the tone for this subject of the name יהוה and His power. אל שדי (El Almighty)[51] begins to explain why He brought the plagues on Egypt. He says,

> For if by now I had put forth My hand and struck you and your people with pestilence, you would then have been cut off from the earth.
>
> EXODUS 9:15

But then יהוה says something that is both revelatory and radical about Pharaoh, king of Egypt:

---

[49] El Emet, Psalms 31:5 in English and 31:6 in the Hebrew Scriptures.
[50] El Gimuloat, Jeremiah 51:56.
[51] El Shaddai, Exodus 6:3.

But, indeed, for this reason I have allowed you to remain, in order to show you My power and in order to proclaim My name through all the earth.

EXODUS 9:16

The purpose of the power displayed in Egypt was to proclaim the name יהוה! So what is the connection between the Holy Name and divine power? Scripture teaches us that when יהוה gave His name to His people, it was understood that power would also come. Where יהוה places His name you can expect power!

Behold, I am going to send an angel before you to guard you along the way and to bring you into the place which I have prepared. Be on your guard before him and obey his voice; do not be rebellious toward him, for he will not pardon your transgression, since My name is in him.

EXODUS 23:20–21

Who is this angel that was sent to guide the people? We do not know his name; but we do know that he carried the name יהוה, which had the authority and power of אל גבור (Strong El).[52] The people were told that if they obeyed the voice of the angel who carried the name, they would have victory over their enemies. This is the power of the One who sent the angel and who promised that if they listened to his voice and obeyed, He would be the One who is called האל הנתן נקמת (The El Who Executes Vengeance).[53]

But if you truly obey his voice and do all that I say, then I will be an enemy to your enemies and an adversary to your adversaries. For My angel will go before you and bring you into the land of the Amorites, the Hittites, the Perizzites, the Canaanites,

---

[52] El Gibbor, Isaiah 9:6 in English and 9:5 in the Hebrew Scriptures.
[53] Ha El Hanoten Nekamoat, 2 Samuel 22:48.

the Hivites and the Jebusites; and I will completely destroy them.

EXODUS 23:22–23

Would you agree that the angel that had the name of our Heavenly Father also had His power and authority? Would you agree that the authority of the name also brought the power? There is power connected to the name!

This brings me to an important question: "What is the expectation of those who speak in this name?" Since it is a powerful name, we should expect to see power in those who carry it. He is the One who is called by the name that encourages me: האל המאזרני חיל (The El Who Girds Me with Strength).[54]

In 2002, as I was writing the first study about the name, titled *For His Name's Sake,* my city of Charlotte, North Carolina, experienced the worst ice storm in the history of the state. More than *two* million homes, *excluding* mine, lost power. One morning during that event I went out to get the paper and saw this headline in *The Charlotte Observer:* "Powerless." The headline reminded me of the power in the name יהוה.

What is the connection between the name and the power? I am convinced that this is the reason I have been studying this topic for the last seven years. Once you learn the name יהוה, you cannot keep it to yourself. There are too many manifestations of the power that follow His name. Unfortunately, there are many people who are experiencing what the fine people of Charlotte experienced. They are disconnected from the source and have become powerless!

I wish I did not need reminders of such an important revelation. But, like most people, I can use a little "note from heaven" every once in a while just to keep me on track. Something happened to me while I was in the midst of our book tour for *A Prayer to Our Father: Hebrew Origins of the Lord's Prayer* which reminded me of the importance of power and the name. In fact, it

---

[54] Ha El Ham'azreni Chayil, Psalms 18:32 in English and 18:33 in the Hebrew Scriptures.

was more like a rebuke than a reminder. My co-author, Nehemia Gordon, asked me to give a joint presentation with him about our book in Colorado Springs. Even though I have had some very significant spiritual experiences in Colorado, I had not thought about the significance of my return there until the morning of my scheduled flight from Charlotte. Of course, it just happened to be a *second* airplane incident that reminded me about the power and the name.

It all started when I assumed that my wife, Andrea, had set the alarm for my 5:15 a.m. wake-up. She had asked me what time I needed to get up just before she went to bed. Not until I woke up at 5:45 a.m. did I remember the problem with making assumptions. Andrea and I worked together to get me to the airport in plenty of time, only to find out that my seat on the plane was not yet assigned. As I watched everybody else board the airplane, I had a bit of an anxious feeling until the dreaded announcement from the ticket agent came through loud and clear. Supposedly there was a problem with the battery on the plane and they were "checking it out." Twenty minutes later I watched passengers get off the plane and make arrangements to take other flights. Eventually they made the announcement that the flight was cancelled. I would have to reschedule my trip for the next day.

This event caused me to take a step back and ask if it meant anything. Of course, if you know me, you understand that this is just the way I operate. There have been entirely too many situations to count when circumstances on earth have tried to teach me something from אלוה ממעל (Eloah From Above).[55] Prior to the battery problem on my scheduled flight I had a very casual attitude regarding the meeting in Colorado Springs. When I returned home from the airport I realized that I had made a crucial mistake. I had not asked אלהים עזר לי (Elohim My Helper)[56] to help me with my message for the people in Colorado.

---

[55] Eloah Mimma'al, Job 3:4.
[56] Elohim Ozer Li, Psalms 54:4 in English and 54:6 in the Hebrew Scriptures.

46

After returning home I reached for my Hebrew Bible and prayed and asked forgiveness for my arrogance and self-reliance. That is when I was lead to three words in my Hebrew Bible that changed my attitude and my message. אנכי יהוה אלהיך *"I am* יהוה *your Elohim."*[57] These three words in Hebrew translate into five words in English. It was the first time I noticed that the *"your"* after *"Elohim"* is singular and not plural in Hebrew. Even though יהוה was speaking to millions of people, he was also saying to the individual, "I am יהוה *your* Elohim."[58] This one small revelation, combined with the powerless airplane that could not take me to Colorado, ultimately spurred me to continue to work on writing this *second* attempt to explain this awesome name. I had His name in my possession for the presentation, yet I had disconnected the power source. There was something wrong with the battery connection. It was me! I ended up changing my message for the people and shared the power of the name יהוה. I considered this an intervention from heaven and it is one of the reasons you are reading this information on earth.

As Nehemia and I traveled around the country presenting our book *A Prayer to Our Father: Hebrew Origins of the Lord's Prayer,* we both felt the conviction that the name of our Heavenly Father needed to be shared. In fact, we made a conscious decision to place the name in our book for all to see and speak. The problem was that many people from Jewish, Christian, and also Messianic backgrounds were a bit uncomfortable with our practice of pronouncing the name יהוה. During one of our presentations, after I spoke the name יהוה, a Jewish rabbi got up and left the presentation. He later explained to our host that my speaking the name made him too uncomfortable.

During a separate interaction with a Messianic man, he explained that though he really liked our presentation he did not agree with us speaking the name of the One whom he called

---

[57] Exodus 20:2

[58] אלהיך (*Eloheka*) is a noun in construct form with a singular suffix.

Hashem.[59] He had been taught that the name was not to be spoken and, in fact, it was not even necessary to know it. As I was discussing the issue with him, Nehemia suggested that I let him see the name printed in my Hebrew Bible. As I was about to show it to him, he quickly stood up and prepared to leave the room. After calming him down and agreeing not to show him the name, he reluctantly sat back on the sofa. The sad part of the interaction with this man was that, by his own admission of difficult personal circumstances, he needed the power of the name! He had an opportunity to see for himself the magnificent, all-powerful name of the Almighty Creator of the universe with his own two eyes, but tradition prohibited him from even looking at it. He was convinced that the tradition of men trumped the truth about the name, so he missed an encounter with the power it carries!

When the people of אלהים קדשים (Holy Elohim)[60] return to knowing and *sanctifying* His name, they will experience His power.

> Nevertheless He saved them for the sake of His name, that He might make His power known.
>
> PSALMS 106:8

---

[59] Hashem is a Hebrew term that simply means "the name." It is used by many Jews today when referring to יהוה.

[60] Elohim Kedoshim, Joshua 24:19-20.

לֹא לָנוּ יְהוָה לֹא לָנוּ כִּי לְשִׁמְךָ תֵּן כָּבוֹד עַל חַסְדְּךָ עַל אֲמִתֶּךָ

Not to us, O יהוה, not to us, but to Your name give glory because of Your lovingkindness, because of Your truth.

PSALMS 115:1

ה

HEY

CHAPTER FIVE

HIDE OR SEEK?

Having access to valuable information about the name of our Heavenly Father is like knowing where people are hiding while playing the game of hide-and-seek. This chapter will give you the opportunity to see how the name was concealed and how to reveal it.

One of the most fulfilling effects of my encounter with the holy name יהוה is that I have felt like a free man. I have sensed the shackles of confusion and doubt falling from my hands so I can lift them to the One called אל אמונה (El Who Is Faithful).[61] This is one of the many benefits of learning His name. My desire is that many others will also find this truth and be set free to worship. For this to happen some may have to face serious challenges.

When it comes to the name illustrated on the front cover of this book, there are two words that define our challenge of discovering the truth: *tradition* and *translation*. In order to uncover

---

[61] El Emunah, Deuteronomy 32:4.

49

this awesome and glorious name we will need to deal with this *two-edged* sword. For 1,900 years both governmental and religious organizations have wielded this sword against anyone wanting to proclaim, pronounce, or even publicly pray the Hebrew holy name of our Heavenly Father.

Before I address these *two* challenges I want you to ponder the following scenario. Imagine that I have been invited to a synagogue as a guest speaker by the rabbi. He introduces me as an author, a seminary-trained United Methodist pastor, and a man who has studied with a Hebrew Bible scholar from Jerusalem for the last several years. He then explains to the congregation that I have researched the name of "Adonai" in depth. After my sensational introduction I tell them that the personal name of the One they call "Adonai" or "Hashem" is not to be spoken by anyone; then I read the following verse from my Hebrew Tanach and translate it into English as proof:

> "My name shall no more be named in the mouth of any man of Judah. . . ."
>
> JEREMIAH 44:26 (King James Version)

In this hypothetical situation I would probably see some affirmative nods from the Jewish brothers and sisters in attendance. Some people would not open their Tanach to read the verse and verify if what I said was accurate. Others might open their holy book, but leave the interpretation to the "expert." As sad as this may sound, it happens every Shabbat in many synagogues, and every Sunday in many churches around the world.

If you read this verse and its context you will immediately realize that my interpretation is faulty at best. You will notice that יהוה is speaking to a specific group of people who live in a specific place and have been doing something specific with their vows in His name. You will also notice that this particular group of people has been designated for suffering and death because of their actions. If you read the entire chapter you will understand why יהוה is prohibiting these specific people from *invoking* His name. If you read the whole book of Jeremiah you may be surprised to find that He actually *wants* both Jews and Gentiles to learn to vow in the name יהוה. Before we move on, please open your Hebrew Tanach or English Bible and at least read the whole verse, if not the entire chapter.

Now let's address the *two* challenges. I must say that whether you are Jewish or Christian this will be difficult to work through. But you will be blessed if you face it with an open mind and heart. These challenges deal with the familiar titles *Adonai* and *LORD*. Making some people a bit uncomfortable is unavoidable. For many, these titles have become a significant part of their faith journey. In fact, some people who regularly say or pray these titles actually think of them as personal names. But we must remember that they are titles, not names, and they are used because of *tradition—not truth*. The great news is that we have not lost the original true information.

In this chapter we will look at the *tradition* of using the title *Adonai* and why it was adopted as a substitute for the name. In the next chapter we will look at the *translation* issue as it pertains to the word *LORD*. Then we will combine the *two* challenges in a section on *traditional translation confusion*.

ADONAI

It is a well-known fact that most Jews will not speak the personal name יהוה, even if they know how to pronounce it. And Christians, even after they learn it, may not want to pronounce it for fear of being ostracized for getting too close to "the Jews and their law." This is an example of the power of what *The Fiddler on the Roof* calls *"Tradition, Tradition!"* I have to respect the many wonderful and meaningful traditions that the Jewish people have handed down over the centuries. However, when these traditions cause people to *miss the truth* they must be challenged and, yes, even changed.

When a Jewish boy prepares for his Bar Mitzvah by reading the Torah Scroll and sees the Hebrew name יהוה, his rabbi will tell him to say *Adonai*. If the boy has the chutzpah to ask why he should substitute a title for the actual name written in the text, he may simply hear, *"Tradition, my son."* If he receives a beautiful copy of The Stone Edition Chumash as a gift after the ceremony, he will have in his possession the *traditional* Jewish answer to this question. Right in the front of the book there is a section titled: Pronouncing the Names of God. Once he reads it he is supposed to stop asking questions and accept the traditional answer.

> During prayer, or when a blessing is recited, or when a Torah verse is read, the Four-Letter Name should be pronounced as if it were spelled אֲדֹנָי a-do-nai, The Name that identifies God as the Master of All. At other times, it should be pronounced השם *Hashem,* literally "the Name."[62]

The Ban on Pronouncing the Name

When did this tradition of not speaking the name יהוה begin? There is an interesting verse that shows that His name was "banned," at least by the Samaritans, as early as 700 BCE; this means they knew and feared יהוה, but called on the name of a Canaanite deity instead of using the authentic name of the Creator of the universe.

> But every nation still made gods of its own and put them in the houses of the high places which the people of Samaria had made. . . . the men of Hamath made Ashima. . . . They feared יהוה and served their own gods according to the custom of the nations from among whom they had been carried away into exile.
>
> 2 KINGS 17:29-30, 33

---

[62] The Stone Edition Chumash, edited by Rabbi Nosson Scherman/Rabbi Meir Zlotowitz. Brooklyn, New York: Mesorah Publications, 2001.

I find it curious that they knew and feared יהוה, but they worshipped Ashima (אֲשִׁימָא). Interestingly, the Samaritans today call יהוה *shema* (שְׁמָא), which means *name* in Aramaic, and the Jews call Him *Hashem,* which means *the name* in Hebrew. Ashima, Shema, and Hashem are just too similar in sound for me to call יהוה any of these names. What do you think?

For the answer about when the official ban on pronouncing the name was adopted by the Jewish people, we must go outside the boundaries of Scripture, since we can easily establish that the Scriptures teach us to know, speak, pray, sing, proclaim, sanctify, and even vow in the Holy Name יהוה. I have had to venture into the unfamiliar waters of Jewish literature to find the witness of this tradition. Many scholars simply say that the Jews believe the name is too holy to speak. That is only part of the reason for the ban on the use of the name. Just after Hanukkah[63] in 2002 the following information was shared with me as I was researching this topic. The Talmud[64] actually gives us a glimpse of the source of this tradition:

> The Grecian government had forbidden the mention of God's name by the Israelites, and when the Hasmoneans became strong and defeated them [the Greeks] they [the Jews] ordained that they should mention the name of God even on bonds. . . . and when the Sages [rabbis] heard of it they said, "Tomorrow this man will pay his debt and the bond will be thrown on a dunghill," and they stopped them.
>
> TALMUD ROSH HASHANAH 18:b

This information about the Hasmoneans is worthy of further reflection. If you have not had the opportunity to do so, I

---

[63] A Jewish eight-day celebration commemorating the rededication of the Temple.

[64] The Talmud is a Jewish commentary on Scripture. It has two components: the Mishnah (c. 200 C.E.), the first written compendium of Judaism's Oral Law, and the Gemara (c. 500 C.E.), a discussion of the Mishnah and related writings that often deals with other subjects and expounds broadly on the Tanach.

encourage you to read the books of First and Second Maccabees in any Catholic Bible. Though these books are not considered "Scripture" by Jews or Protestants, they give a helpful historic picture of the efforts of the Seleucid Greeks to hellenize the Jewish people around 168 B.C.E. We know there were at least three things that Antiochus IV Epiphanes forbade the Jews to do. He outlawed the observance of the Sabbath, the circumcision of children, and speaking the name יהוה. He also desecrated the Temple by sacrificing swine to Zeus on the altar and forcing people to eat the unclean meat. Antiochus knew that if he was going to be successful in defeating the Jews, he would need to take away their identity as the people of אל אלהי ישראל (El Elohim of Israel).[65] Everything that gave the Jewish people security, confidence, or identity was under attack.

From 168 until 165 B.C.E. many Jewish people were unable to resist the hellenization. The Hasmoneans, under the leadership of Judas Maccabaeus, resisted the Greeks and were finally able to defeat Antiochus and his army. However, the process of bringing the people back to true worship was a challenge. The very center of worship was destroyed, and great damage had been done to the hearts of the people.

In an attempt to revive them, the Hasmoneans knew the name יהוה had to be restored. The early Hasmonean rulers were all Sadducees, but the rabbinical religious leaders, who were Pharisees, opposed them.[66] The Sadducees, loyal to written Scripture, still used the name יהוה, even on business contracts. The Pharisees did not agree with this practice, so a battle began and continued for years.[67] The rabbis had a legitimate reverence for the Holy Name and they felt it was too holy to be used on contracts. Their concern was what might happen to these legal documents once the contracts were completed. As mentioned in the Talmud reference above, the sages said, "Tomorrow this man will pay his debt and the bond [contract]

---

[65] El Elohe Yisrael, Genesis 33:20.
[66] Josephus, *Antiquities* 13.10.6; *Babylonian Talmud, Kiddushin* 66a.
[67] Nehemia Gordon, "The Pronunciation of the Name," www.Karaite-Korner.org.

will be thrown on a dunghill,' and they stopped them." Ultimately, the ancient rabbis took the issue too far and disallowed the pronunciation and proclamation of the name of our Heavenly Father by His people.

I must acknowledge that there is still valid debate over how widespread and for how long the ban on the name existed. It is safe to say that for at least 300 years there were pockets of people who obeyed the ban and others who disobeyed.

In the late first century we have historical evidence of the prohibition of speaking the name from the famous Jewish historian Flavius Josephus, who was born in 36 C.E. and died sometime shortly after 100 C.E. In reference to the revelation of the name יהוה to Moses at the burning bush he says:

> Whereupon God declared to him his holy name, which had never been discovered to men before; concerning which it is not lawful for me to say any more.[68]

Josephus seems to be testifying that he had, in fact, spoken the name יהוה at some point in his lifetime. However, either through a religious or governmental ban on the pronunciation of the name, Josephus says: *". . . it is not lawful for me to say any more."* Josephus obviously has more to say, but is forbidden from doing so. It is as though one day it was okay to pronounce the name and then, because of external prohibitions, it was forbidden. This ban may coincide with the destruction of the Temple in 70 C.E., which Josephus witnessed and wrote about. The exact time and reason for the ban is uncertain; however, the fact that such a ban on the name יהוה existed is undeniable.

Many scholars argue that Josephus was a rule-abiding Pharisee and therefore followed pharisaical practices and prohibitions. There is also much debate about his religious allegiance. The

---

[68] Josephus, Flavius. *The Complete Works of Josephus,* translated by William Whiston, Kregel Publications, Grand Rapids, Michigan, 1981, pages 50-51.

Pharisees were not the only ones to ban the use of the name. Josephus reports that there were three main groups in Second Temple Judaism: the Pharisees, the Sadducees, and the Essenes.[69] The Essenes were a very close-knit group of people who kept to themselves. They wrote what are now called the Dead Sea Scrolls.[70] One scroll, called *Rule of the Community,* outlines the rules and regulations of how to live as an Essene. An important prohibition mentioned in this document clearly states:

> Anyone who speaks aloud the M[ost] Holy Name of God, [whether in . . .] or in cursing or as a blurt in time of trial or for any other reason, or while he is reading a book or praying, is to be expelled, never again to return to the body of the community. (1QS 6:27-7:2)[71]

What a privilege it has been to work so closely with Nehemia Gordon, who was a translator for the Dead Sea Scrolls project under the direction of the world-renowned Hebrew scholar Dr. Emanuel Tov. Like many of the Dead Sea Scrolls, part of this scroll is damaged and some of the passage cannot be read. It is clear, however, that this is a prohibition forbidding the use of our Heavenly Father's name even in prayer. The punishment for using the name יהוה was the most severe the Essenes could administer: permanent expulsion from the community.[72]

The Essenes knew and revered the name. They even made a distinction in their writings by using Paleo-Hebrew letters rather than Assyrian letters when they wrote it. When this book was in its early stages I was invited to the ordination service of a close friend. As I entered the convention center and started up the escalator, I

---

[69] Josephus, Flavius. *The Complete Works of Josephus,* page 274.

[70] The Dead Sea Scrolls are ancient biblical and community writings that were discovered in caves in Israel in 1947.

[71] First cave at Qumran, column 6, line 27 through column 7, line 2 of the Manual of Discipline.

[72] Nehemia Gordon, "The Pronunciation of the Name," www.Karaite-Korner.org.

looked out the large windows and something caught my attention. Hanging on a building across the street was a very large banner displaying Hebrew letters. In the middle of the Hebrew text was the four-letter name of our Heavenly Father written in Paleo-Hebrew ⟨Hebrew⟩ just like the writing on the silver scrolls I mentioned in Chapter Two. The Dead Sea Scrolls Exhibition was in town and the mammoth-sized banner was featuring one of the many scrolls found by a young Arab boy in 1947.

To no avail, I tried to explain to my family the excitement of seeing the name publicly displayed in the ancient Paleo-Hebrew script. The expressions on their faces communicated something like, "Here he goes again." How could I blame them? Trying to explain the significance of His name while riding up an escalator was not the best learning environment. However, the opening hymn of the service provided a much better opportunity: "Holy God We Praise Thy Name."[73]

As everyone else was singing, I imagined myself stopping the music and asking, "What name are we to praise?" I wanted to lead everyone out of the service and across the street to the Dead Sea Scrolls Exhibition so I could explain the different looking Paleo-Hebrew letters ⟨Hebrew⟩ that represented "Thy Name." I wanted them to know why the Essenes wrote this name differently and prohibited its pronunciation. Unfortunately, my desire to teach people about His name probably would have gotten me ushered out of the ordination service; not to mention the embarrassment it would have caused my family as they tried to explain to my friend why I wasn't present for his ordination. I must confess, though, that I took a short break from the festivities to get a closer look at the banner.

There are so many things we can learn about the Essene community from the astounding discovery of the Dead Sea Scrolls. The key point here is that there were *two* out of three religious groups (Pharisees and Essenes) who kept a "tradition" that banned the name from being spoken. The majority eventually prevailed and

---

[73] The Covenant Hymnal: *A Worshipbook*, #19.

the tradition became so effective that even today people sing hymns such as "Praising Thy Holy Name" without the faintest idea what that name is.

The source of this tradition points to the Greeks, who were afraid of the name יהוה being spoken by the people. We should not be surprised since יהוה had already said,

"I am a great King," says יהוה of hosts, "and My name is feared among the nations."
MALACHI 1:14

At some point after 70 C.E. the name was banned completely, and those who used it could even be punished by death.

In approximately 136 C.E. a man named Rabbi Hanina b. Teradion was put to death during the reign of the evil Emperor Hadrian for publicly speaking the name יהוה. He was reportedly wrapped in a Torah Scroll and set on fire.[74]

They then brought up R. Hanina b. Teradion and asked him, 'Why hast thou occupied thyself with the Torah?' He replied, 'Thus the Lord my God [יהוה my Elohim] commanded me.' At once they sentenced him to be burnt. . . . The punishment of being burnt came upon him because he pronounced the Name in its full spelling. Why then was he punished? Because he was pronouncing the Name in public.
BABYLONIAN TALMUD AVODAH ZARAH 17a–18b

Did you catch those *two* words *"full spelling?"* More about that later. Sadly, the religious leaders of the day supported this ban

---

[74] "Straightaway they took hold of him, wrapt him in the Scroll of the Law, placed bundles of branches round him and set them on fire" (Babylonian Talmud Avodah Zarah 17a-18b).

and continued to enforce it. The modern Mishnah Berurah[75] reveals the final development of the banning of the name:

> It is forbidden to read the glorious and terrible name as it is written, as the sages said, "He that pronounces the name as it is written has no portion in the world to come." Therefore it must be read as if it were written Adonai.
>
> MISHNAH BERURAH 5:2

This next source of information about the ban is found as early as the third century C.E. in the Mishnah Tractate of Sanhedrin:

> The following have no portion in the world to come, Abba Saul says: Also one who pronounces the divine name as it is written.
>
> MISHNAH SANHEDRIN 10:1

This means that around 200 C.E. there was a clear mandate from historical Jewish authority that the name of the Creator must not be pronounced. If a person considers the Mishnah to be authoritative, I can understand why he or she would refrain from using the name. Imagine if your Bible taught that you were going to miss out on eternity if you pronounced the name of our Heavenly Father. Unfortunately, many people have taken the tradition of men and made it authoritative, so that 1,900 years later the ban persists!

It is particularly interesting that in the early rabbinic period the name was limited in its pronunciation, but not banned. In other words, before 70 C.E. the name was spoken in the Temple service, but a substitute word was used in daily conversation and personal devotion. The following reference from the Talmud confirms this rule of substitution:

---

[75] The Mishnah is a collection of oral interpretations of the Torah. It was compiled by Rabbi Yehudah Prince and others around 200 C.E.

In the Sanctuary the Name was pronounced as
written; but beyond its confines a substituted Name
was employed.

SOT. VII 6

This helps solve the mystery of the prohibition against
pronouncing the name. Clearly, the name יהוה was pronounced by
the priests, but not among the people. It was not that it was too
holy to pronounce, as many scholars state. The name was considered so holy that it was reserved for a holy service. The common
people heard the name pronounced, but were prohibited from using it themselves. Now we are getting closer to the fiery heart of the
matter. There were three occasions when the priests publicly pronounced the potent and powerful name יהוה. The following comes
from a very helpful book about the teachings of the rabbinic sages:

> The Tetragrammaton was included in the priestly
> benediction which was daily pronounced in the Tem-
> ple. It was also used by the High Priest on the Day of
> Atonement, when he made the threefold confession
> of sins on behalf of himself, the priests and the com-
> munity. The third occasion is described in this man-
> ner: 'Thus did he say: O JHVH, Thy people, the
> House of Israel, have committed iniquity, have trans-
> gressed, have sinned before Thee. I beseech Thee by
> the Name JHVH, make thou atonement for the ini-
> quities and for the transgressions and for the sins
> wherein Thy people, the House of Israel, have com-
> mitted iniquity, have transgressed and sinned before
> Thee; as it is written in the Torah of Thy servant
> Moses, saying: "For on this day shall atonement be
> made for you, to cleanse you; from all your sins shall
> ye be clean before JHVH" (Lev. xvi. 30).[76]

---

[76] Cohen, Abraham. *Everyman's Talmud: The Major Teachings of the Rabbinic Sages.*
Schocken Books, New York, 1995, pages 24-25.

Obviously, the name was pronounced with regularity by the priests and heard by the people. In fact, additional information is included in the Talmud indicating the people's response when they heard the priests speak the name:

> And when the priests and the people that stood in the Court heard the glorious and revered Name pronounced freely out of the mouth of the High Priest, in holiness and purity, they knelt and prostrated themselves, falling on their faces, and exclaiming: 'Blessed be His glorious, sovereign Name forever and ever'.
>
> JOMA VI. 2

As further testimony, there also seems to have been a different process of speaking the name.[77] It was initially spoken in a loud voice; then eventually spoken in a more quiet voice. The following *two* references in the Talmud give us this witness. The first is from a testimony from R. Tarphon, who was a member of a priestly family:

> On one occasion I followed my uncles on to the dais, and I inclined my ear to catch what the High Priest said. I heard him cause the Name to be drowned by the singing of his brother-priests.
>
> KIDDUSHIN 71a

> At first the High Priest used to proclaim the Name in a loud voice; but when dissolute men multiplied, he proclaimed it in a low tone.
>
> JERUSALEM TALMUD, JOMA 40d

---

[77] "Our Rabbis taught: At first [God's] *twelve-lettered Name* used to be entrusted to all people" (Soncino translation of Kiddushin 71a). Thanks Nehemia!

The reference regarding this different way of pronouncing the name provides a similar picture of what happened with the four-letter name יהוה. Even after being restricted to the Temple, the name was still known and used. But over time the priests stopped proclaiming it in a loud voice and began whispering it so the people couldn't hear it. Now the use of the name has been discontinued and limited to those "in the know" who practically have kept it under lock and key. Instead of letting people like you and me have access to this glorious and revered name, they have provided a substitute title that is supposed to satisfy those of us who want the original.

The religious leaders still had a problem because *the name was right there in the written sacred text for all to see!* The rabbinic authorities realized that they had to decide what to tell the people to do when they came across this name יהוה that appeared 6,828 times in their Hebrew Scriptures. I must admit that what they came up with is ingenious. They simply found a Hebrew word meaning "lord" or "master" which appears next to the name יהוה 297 times in the Hebrew Scriptures. The word is *Adonai*. They told the people to say *Adonai* instead of יהוה. What a creative idea! What a sad result!

People like Moses, Joshua, Gideon, Samson, David, Isaiah, and Jeremiah—and especially Ezekiel[78]—included this title *Adonai* as the first of *two* Hebrew words on numerous occasions when speaking to or about our Heavenly Father. They would say or pray אדני יהוה (*Adonai* יהוה) when addressing Him. They employed the Hebrew word *Adonai* as a perfectly appropriate *introductory title* for the majestic One named יהוה. Not one of these men would have ever considered *Adonai* to be His personal name!

I find it particularly fascinating that only one time in all of the Hebrew Scriptures, through the prophet Ezekiel, does יהוה actually use the title *Adonai* when referring to Himself without including His personal name יהוה:

---

[78] Of the 297 examples of the title *Adonai* directly next to יהוה, 210 are found in the book of Ezekiel.

> Son of man, prophesy and say, 'Thus says Adonai . . .'

EZEKIEL 21:9

I can imagine the second-century scribe or rabbi who found this reference saying, *"Eureka! I have found justification for the new translation tradition of using the title Adonai rather than the banned name יהוה."* However, I am sure that same scribe or rabbi lost some of his enthusiasm after he examined the other four references in this context. They all contain the exact same wording and show that the people were calling יהוה *Adonai*. Notice the wording in Ezekiel 18:25, 18:29, 33:17, and 33:20. You will see the following in all four examples:

> 'The way of Adonai is not right.'

Since this was how the people of that day referred to יהוה, saying His *"way is not right,"* what did He do? Speaking through the prophet Ezekiel and employing the same terminology the people used, יהוה said, *"Thus says Adonai . . ."* Does anyone else find that to be clever? The book of Ezekiel, which uses the title *Adonai* right next to יהוה more than any other book, has a group of self-righteous people who use the title *Adonai* (Lord) *in place of* His name יהוה four different times.[79] It sounds quite familiar. I am sure some people will react to the information in this book saying, *"The way of the Lord is not right; our way is better."* I just hope this is not your approach to what you are learning. Unfortunately, the young Jewish boy with his new Chumash may never choose to question the tradition of replacing the name יהוה with the title *Adonai*.

The ancient Jewish religious authorities chose the Hebrew word *Adonai* as the substitute for the name יהוה and passed that same *tradition* down to Christian translators. In the next chapter we will evaluate how well the Christian translators did as disciples of

---

[79] It should be noted that there are 137 places throughout the Tanach where *Adonai* is used in reference to יהוה. However, *Adonai* is always a title, not a personal name.

their Jewish teachers. Did they find a way to keep "the Jewish law" of concealing the name יהוה by providing an acceptable substitute? Continue this journey of discovery with me and we will find the answer.

וַיִּקְרְאוּ בַסֵּפֶר בְּתוֹרַת הָאֱלֹהִים מְפֹרָשׁ וְשׂוֹם שֶׂכֶל
וַיָּבִינוּ בַּמִּקְרָא

They read in the book in the Torah of Elohim, translating to give the sense so that they understood the meaning.

NEHEMIAH 8:8 (Keith Johnson Version)

ו

VAV

CHAPTER SIX

LOST IN TRANSLATION

Venturing into the issues surrounding Bible translation is not a simple task. As you begin this chapter keep in mind the famous Italian adage: *Traduttore, traditore,* which means "the translator is a traitor." This phrase is particularly relevant to the process of translating or transliterating the name יהוה into the English language.

Because certain circumstances often seem to line up with what I consider to be my calling, I find myself more aware of what is happening around me. On the day I decided that I would avoid dealing with the arduous task of writing about English Bible history, the Associated Press published the following report:

Top-selling Bible in North America to be Revised

The top-selling Bible in North America will undergo its first revision in 25 years, modernizing the language in some sections and promising to re-open a contentious debate about changing gender terms in the sacred text. The New International Version, the Bible of choice for conservative evangelicals, will be revised to reflect changes in English usage and advances in biblical scholarship, it was announced Tuesday. The revision is scheduled to be completed late next year and published in 2011.

"We want to reach English speakers across the globe with a Bible that is accurate, accessible and that speaks to its readers in a language they can understand," said Keith Danby, global president and CEO of Biblica, a Colorado Springs, Colorado based Christian ministry that holds the NIV copyright.[80]

As soon as I read the article I knew I would not be able to avoid the inevitable conviction and realized that more work would be necessary. How could I write about the translation of the Hebrew name of our Heavenly Father without giving some history of the English translation of the Bible that conceals His name? After hearing about this new version of the Bible, I decided to address the topic in an abbreviated form. My focus is the origins of the English Old Testament rather than the New Testament, since the *sanctified* name יהוה appears only in the Hebrew text. The way the New Testament handles the name יהוה is also a fascinating study, but that topic is beyond the scope of this book.

The Old Testament, with all its power and revelation, was originally written and preserved in the Hebrew language. Around 200 B.C.E. it was translated into Greek, which had become the dominant language in that part of the world. This ancient version of the Hebrew Scriptures was known as the Septuagint. According to legend, it was translated in Alexandria by 70 Jewish scholars; hence the name "Septuagint," commonly abbreviated LXX.

---

[80] Published September 2, 2009 by Eric Gorski, AP Religion Writer.

The Greek version of the Old Testament supplanted the Hebrew Scriptures for Greek-speaking Christians, but it never replaced the Hebrew Scriptures for the Jewish community. Sadly, the Greek language cannot do justice to the power of revelation regarding the Hebrew name יהוה.

In the year 382 Pope Damasus commissioned a man named Jerome to translate the Bible into Latin, the language of the people at the time. In 385 Jerome was forced to leave Rome because of his translation work and he eventually settled in Bethlehem. There he studied under a Jewish rabbi who helped him with his Hebrew proficiency. Eventually Jerome translated the entire "Old Testament" into Latin as part of what is commonly called the Latin Vulgate. The word *vulgate* basically means "the common speech of a people; the vernacular." The technical definition comes from the Latin language, feminine past participle of *vulgāre,* to make known to all, from *vulgus,* the common people. The Latin Vulgate was the official Bible of the Roman Catholic Church for approximately 1,000 years.

In 1378 John Wycliffe finally took action against the official Church position on translation; he wanted English speakers to be able to read the Scriptures. Wycliffe's first handwritten portion of the Bible was produced in an effort to counter a teaching that he felt was contrary to the Bible. Wycliffe and his group, called the Lollards, translated many manuscripts from Latin into English. After his death, Wycliffe's teachings were condemned and he was officially denounced as a heretic by the Roman Catholic Church.

One of Wycliffe's disciples was Jon Hus (1369-1415). He actively promoted the earlier work of Wycliffe and his process of translating the Latin Vulgate into English. The problem for the Roman Church leaders at the time was that they did not want the common folks to find out that the practices of the Church were contrary to the teaching of Scripture. They thought the best way to keep the people from the truth was to not allow them to read the Bible for themselves. Jon Hus did not agree and openly opposed the Church. He was ultimately condemned as a heretic and sentenced to be burned at the stake because he refused to recant.

Some claim the Pope ordered that Wycliffe's English version of the Bible be used for kindling. Whether or not this part of the story is factual can be debated, but the symbolism of English pages of the Bible causing his death is certainly true.

The martyrdom of Jon Hus started a firestorm of sorts because the desire for English translations of Scripture clashed with the Church's prohibition against making the Bible available to the common people. Several men, including Thomas Linacre, John Colet, Erasmus, and William Tyndale continued the practice of making translated portions of the Bible available, even though the threat of death persisted for anyone in possession of an unauthorized English translation. When the printing press was invented in Mainz, Germany, in the 1450s it only added fuel to the fire. The first book printed on this new invention was a Latin edition of the Scriptures called the Gutenberg Bible.

Myles Coverdale translated the Old Testament and the New Testament into English, making his the first complete Bible in the English language. This Bible was printed on October 4, 1535, and is known as the Coverdale Bible. However, Coverdale's translation of the Old Testament came from the Latin Vulgate and not directly from the Hebrew text. In 1537 John Rogers produced the first English Bible translated directly from Hebrew.

In 1539 at the request of King Henry VIII, the Archbishop of Canterbury, Thomas Cranmer, hired Myles Coverdale to print the "Great Bible." This became the first English Bible authorized for public use. It was sent to every church in England and chained to the pulpit. Readers were even provided so the illiterate could hear the words of the Bible in plain English for the first time.

Finally in 1611, with the blessing and authority of King James I of England, the renowned "Authorized Version" of the English Bible was introduced. A number of scholars were assembled to translate the entire Old and New Testaments into an English Bible that would be made available to individuals without threat from the government or the Church of England.

The Bible had a beautiful cover illustrated with powerful biblical images and symbols. It is this Bible that first displayed the four Hebrew letters יהוה on the front cover.[81] So what happened? Why is it that in this modern era of advanced biblical scholarship and technology, the name יהוה has been concealed? When the new NIV Bible comes out *that is accurate, accessible and that speaks to its readers in a language they can understand,"* I will be pleasantly surprised if it contains a true and accurate rendering of the most frequently-mentioned and most important name in all of Scripture.

As you continue this journey with me I hope you will be convinced that the *sanctified* name of our Heavenly Father has indeed been revealed *again*. Unfortunately, in both Catholic and Protestant circles, the attitude regarding common people having access to this awesome Hebrew name is the same today as it was in the Dark Ages. History is indeed repeating itself. The Hebrew language has become the English that was banned, and the English version has become the new Latin, which is the only "Authorized Version" for the common man. In order for me to experience all that the name יהוה offers I had to be willing to stand against the present-day prohibition, open my Hebrew Bible and learn the name! Are you willing to do the same?

Translation Troubles

Now that we have addressed some of the history of the English Bible, let's move on to the challenge of translation. From my earliest Christian experience, I was taught that LORD is the Creator's actual name. I also learned that to use any other "name" was inappropriate. I never even made it to the place where I could ask about any *"four-letter Hebrew name"* because I assumed English was the original language of the Bible. The following statement comes from the first Bible I received when I became a Christian at age fifteen:

---

[81] See 1611 King James Version title page,
http://sceti.library.upenn.edu/sceti/printedbooksnew/index.cfm?TextID=kjbible&PagePositi
on=3

The use of any proper name for the one and only
God, as though there were other gods from whom
He had to be distinguished, was discontinued in
Judaism before the Christian era and is entirely
inappropriate for the universal faith of the Christian
Church.[82]

I must admit that I cringe when I read such statements in
light of what I know now. It is sad that so many people have
missed the blessing of knowing the "proper name" of אלי (My
El).[83] I pray that future generations will be taught the scriptural
truth and not what is deemed *appropriate for the universal faith of
the Christian Church.*

Now back to work! The original language of Scripture is not
English. It is still difficult to convince some people that the Bible
was not originally written in the Old English of the King James
Version. Nonetheless, we know that the "Old Testament" was
originally written in Hebrew, with a few sections in Aramaic. The
problem that immediately presents itself is how to translate these
biblical languages into English.

The Greek Lord

I have already referred to the Greek Septuagint, which
replaced the Hebrew Scriptures for those who did not want to go
through the task of learning Hebrew. Unfortunately, the Greek
language could not do honor to the Hebrew name of our Heavenly
Father. In fact, there are no equivalent Greek letters for the four
Hebrew letters of the holy name יהוה. The name appears in the
Hebrew Scriptures 6,828 times, but its Greek "equivalent" occurs
only 6,575 times in the Septuagint. This means that 253 times the
name is either replaced or simply removed.

---

[82] Harper Study Bible, 1978, page v.
[83] Elee, Exodus 15:2.

The Greek word used in place of the name יהוה is κυριος (*kyrios*). The first time the name יהוה occurs in the Hebrew Scriptures is Genesis 2:4. In the Septuagint the name is completely removed from this verse and replaced with θεος (*Theos*), which is the Greek word for God. However, on other occasions, such as Genesis 2:8, the Septuagint uses both κυριος (*kyrios*) and θεος (*Theos*) together for the exact same Hebrew words that are in Genesis 2:4. In both verses the Hebrew uses Elohim and יהוה, but the Greek uses θεος (*Theos*) alone in one verse, and in the other it combines the words κυριος (*kyrios*) and θεος (*Theos*). This is just one of many problems with the Septuagint.

The Jews became disillusioned with the Greek version once it was adopted by the Christian Church. The early Christians began to distance themselves from their Hebrew roots, but they still needed Jewish help when it came to translating the Hebrew Scriptures (once they decided to translate from Hebrew, rather than Greek). They had a dilemma about what do with this prominent Hebrew name. The rabbis were very willing to teach them exactly what to do when they saw the name יהוה.

English translators followed a practice similar to the Jewish custom of writing and saying *Adonai* when they read יהוה. In English they substituted the word LORD. The translators decided to capitalize the word LORD, to distinguish it from the regular word *lord*. In effect, they made a title into a proper name. This is one of the reasons so many people are tied to a title instead of being in love with His name!

It grieves me to think that choices have been made in translations which have kept us from receiving and understanding the gift of the name יהוה. One of those choices was the use of LORD in place of the personal name of our Heavenly Father. I have already mentioned the translation called *The Scriptures,* which comes from the Institute for Scripture Research.[84] This is what they say about the restoration of the name:

---

[84] See Appendix C: Books of Reference for full information.

One of the post-exilic-apostasies of Orthodox Judaism was the avoidance of the Name of the Almighty. Because of this and a similar and continued suppression and substitution of the Name by the Church, much harm was done to the True Worship. When anyone enquires about this he is told: "The name has been translated into English as LORD as was similarly done in other languages." This argument does not hold water. *Giuseppe* in Italian corresponds to Joseph in English; however, *Giuseppe Verdi* cannot be translated as Joseph Green in English, even if that is what it means in English! The proper name of any individual is not translated; it is always transliterated or transcribed in order to approximate its original pronunciation.[85]

What do other English translators of the Bible do with the proper name of our Heavenly Father? Most of them give some explanation to justify their decision; however, what we are learning challenges their "justification." When I was ordained a deacon in the United Methodist Church I received a Bible from my bishop that has a comment worth examining:

Careful readers will notice that here and there in the Old Testament the word LORD (or in certain cases GOD) is printed in capital letters. This represents the traditional manner in English versions of rendering the Divine Name, the "Tetragrammaton" ... following the precedent of the ancient Greek and Latin translators and the long established practice in the reading of the Hebrew Scriptures in the synagogue.[86]

---

[85] *The Scriptures,* pp. xi-xii.

[86] Bruce M. Metzger and Roland E. Murphy. *The New Oxford Annotated Bible,* "To the Reader," page xii.

This may be one of the few times any mention is made of the "root" of the Christian faith in an English Bible. Though I am grateful for this gift, the authors' explanation disturbs me. Does any committee or individual have the authority to decide to follow tradition, precedent, or established practice rather than truth?

Furthermore, in light of the many agendas evident in translation, one would think that the English translators would try not to make the same mistake, unless, of course, they have some of the same agendas. I also find it noteworthy that they validate the practice of our brothers and sisters in the synagogues, where the Holy Scriptures were preserved. Unfortunately, those Scriptures are now often read through the filter of anti-Semitism. Translators tend to pick and choose what fits the tenor of the day, but this is not the way the name יהוה should be handled.

Here is another popular English translator's explanation:

> In the Scriptures, the name of God is most significant and understandably so. It is inconceivable to think of spiritual matters without a proper designation for the Supreme Deity. Thus the most common name for the Deity is God, a translation of the original Elohim. One of the titles for God is Lord, a translation of Adonai. There is yet another name which is particularly assigned to God as His special or proper name, that is, the four letters YHWH (Exodus 3:14 and Isaiah 42:8). This name has not been pronounced by the Jews because of reverence for the great sacredness of the divine name. Therefore, it has been consistently translated LORD. The only exception to this translation of YHWH is when it occurs in immediate proximity to the word Lord, that is, Adonai. In that case it is regularly translated GOD in order to avoid confusion.[87]

---

[87] Spiros Zodhiates, ed. *The Hebrew-Greek Key Study Bible, NASB,* page v.

Is that confusing? It is to me. How can the "most common" name for the "Deity" be *God* if it is used approximately 4,700 times, while the personal name of the "Deity" is used more than 6,800 times? Also, why would the translators of this Bible render *two* different Hebrew words as *Lord?* Furthermore, why would they ever translate the "special or proper name" as *God* if the Scriptures make such a sharp distinction about the name of the "Supreme Deity"? As you can see, translators have made numerous crucial decisions that have kept us from seeing and knowing the name. The following verse demonstrates the "confusion:"

> I prayed to the LORD and said, 'O Lord GOD . . .'
>
> DEUTERONOMY 9:26

The proper name יהוה is first rendered as LORD and then as GOD in the same verse. The translators capitalized the English letters in both cases "in order to avoid confusion." They then use the same English word *Lord* with lower case letters to represent a different Hebrew word, *Adonai,* to make sure that you will not be "confused." In other words, you are supposed to know that if you see LORD or GOD (capital letters) they really don't mean Lord or God at all but are substitutes for the personal name of our Heavenly Father יהוה. There are 291 verses in your English Bible that will confuse you like this.

I suggest you look in your English Bible to see if there is a section explaining the reason for making translation decisions about the name יהוה. Be careful not to get too discouraged, because help is on the way!

To put a little icing on this cake of translation confusion, I would like to share one more issue regarding the English word *Lord.* The English translators actually decided to transliterate a second Hebrew word rather than translate it. This apparently was done in order to avoid confusion with the substitute word LORD. This word is used in our English Bibles 65 times. In fact, it is transliterated and pronounced the same in Hebrew and Greek.[88] It appears in the Hebrew text as בַּעַל (*Ba'al*) and in Greek as Βααλ (*Baal*). It can be translated as "husband," "lord," or "master." In fact, modern Hebrew uses this exact word for the term "husband." Now bear with me as I express my concern about the inconsistency of our dear English Bible translators.

To be truly consistent regarding the translation of Hebrew words, the following two verses should have been rendered like this:

> How long will the hearts of the prophets ever turn back, those who prophesy lies and who prophesy the deceit of their own heart? They plan to make my people forget my name by their dreams that they tell each other, even as their fathers forgot my name for Lord.
>
> JEREMIAH 23:26–27 (Keith Johnson Version)

Please open your English Bible and compare your version with mine. You will notice that 100% of the time the translators find it acceptable to retain this Hebrew word rather than use its English equivalent. For whatever reason—and we now know what it is—the translators retained the Hebrew בַּעַל (*Ba'al*) rather than translate it into what would be, in this case, *Lord* as a proper noun. Why didn't they do the same thing with the Hebrew name יהוה since both are considered proper nouns? Instead of seeing LORD thousands of times in our Bibles we should see the Hebrew name of our Heavenly Father יהוה just like we see the Hebrew name *Ba'al!* I find this inconsistency rather telling!

Now for the cherry on top. When it comes to translation there are always exceptions to the rules, especially when dealing with the name יהוה. There is a verse that, in my opinion, must have caused English translators a real headache over whether or not to use the original Hebrew word or an English equivalent.

---

[88] See Romans 11:4 for the Greek example of Baal.

"It will come about in that day," declares יהוה, "that you will call Me Ishi and will no longer call me Baali."

HOSEA 2:16 (2:18 in the Hebrew Scriptures)

In most English versions *two* of the Hebrew words in this verse are left untranslated. If you go back to Chapter Three you might remember this word איש (*ish*) which can be translated as *man* or *husband*. The *"i"* on the end of *ishi* and *baali* are the first person singular suffix meaning "my." The translators have at least two options for dealing with this word—*Baali* can be rendered as either "my husband" or "my lord." However, the real concern is that it could be translated as "my Lord." To be truly consistent, this is how the verse should have been translated:

"It will come about in that day," declares יהוה, "that you will call Me my husband and will no longer call Me my Lord."

HOSEA 2:16 (2:18 in the Hebrew Scriptures)

Now look at your English translation of this verse. Do you see the problems this would cause? People might actually realize that יהוה is saying that a day is coming when He will no longer be called *my Lord* and instead He will be called *my husband!*

While you think about that, may I offer a little comic relief? The above verse reminds me of the famous phrase regarding my last name by Ray J. Johnson. He becomes annoyed when addressed as "Johnson," and exclaims in a loud voice, *"My name is Raymond J. Johnson, Jr. Now you can call me Ray, or you can call me J, or you can call me Johnny, or you can call me Sonny, or you can call me Junie, or you can call me Ray J, or you can call me RJ, or you can call me RJJ, or you can call me RJJ Jr., but you doesn't hasta call me Johnson!"*

Sometimes I want to say this about the name יהוה. By the end of this study you will learn 80 different Hebrew titles or descriptions that He would prefer for you to call Him; *but you doesn't hasta call him Baal!*

On a more serious note, *Baal* is the name of an ancient Canaanite deity. In fact, this pagan deity became a snare to the Israelites and caused judgment to fall on them because they followed the Canaanites in their false worship. We find many references throughout the Old Testament to the Israelites worshipping Baal.[89] They believed that Baal was "lord" of the earth, so it was an easy transition to take the title of a false god and use it as a substitute for the name of our Heavenly Father. Can you understand why this might be offensive to the real Creator of the heavens and the earth who has a personal name?

Some people might consider it an overreaction to make such a big deal about using the word Baal, since it can be translated as *husband* or *Lord.* They would say that *Baal* or *Lord* is an appropriate substitute for the name יהוה. There are *two* very interesting examples of Israelite kings using the name Baal as a substitute for the holy name יהוה. King Saul actually named one of his sons *Ishbaal,* which means "man of Baal" (1 Chronicles 8:33 and 9:39). Interestingly, the prophet Samuel called this son of Saul *Ishbosheth,* meaning "man of shame."[90] Ishbosheth, or *Ishbaal* as he was called in Chronicles, actually ruled as king of Israel with this "shameful name" for two years.

In the second example King David went so far as to acknowledge that יהוה "breaks forth," but named the place where it happened "Baal breaks forth" (2 Samuel 5:20). In both cases the kings used the word *Baal* but were referring to יהוה. How did יהוה feel about being called Baal? Hosea goes on to say:

> For I will remove the names of the Baals from her mouth, so that they will be mentioned by their names no more.
>
> HOSEA 2:17 (2:19 in the Hebrew Scriptures)

---

[89] See 1 Kings 16:31, 22:53, 2 Kings 10:19-23 as examples of Baal worship.
[90] See 2 Samuel chapters 2-4.

When people say, "It really doesn't matter what I call Him because He knows what I mean," I think it is appropriate to challenge them to reconsider their position. If we can know His name—and we can—then why not use it rather than replacing it with an unworthy title? After all, how would you or I feel if we had a friend who knew our names but consistently refused to use them when speaking to us or about us?

Traditional Interpretation Confusion

In order to really get to the core of the tradition and translation challenges, I will address some long-standing biblical interpretations. The traditional explanation by Jewish and Christian scholars of *two* key passages regarding the name has fueled this fire of confusion in synagogues and churches. It is my position that these *two* biblical passages have been historically misinterpreted and, therefore, have been used as "proof texts" to enforce the ban on speaking the name יהוה.

The first verse I want to delve into comes from, arguably, the most well-known event in the entire "Old Testament." If I asked anyone who is even slightly acquainted with the Bible about this event, he or she would probably acknowledge at least some familiarity with the context and might even be able to quote the verse. I am referring to the Third Commandment given on Mount Sinai when the famous Ten Commandments were spoken by יהוה.

> You shall not take the name יהוה your Elohim in vain, for יהוה will not leave him unpunished who takes His name in vain.
>
> EXODUS 20:7

This is a serious matter that bears directly on our relationship with אל נשא (El Who Forgives).[91] I can understand why some people would want to steer clear of speaking the Divine

---

[91] El Nose', Psalms 99:8.

Name just from reading this one command, unless, of course, it is in conflict with the rest of scriptural teaching. This is exactly the problem with the traditional interpretation of this commandment. A good deal of confusion arises from the English translation; we will deal with that over the next few pages.

Have you ever heard a Jewish rabbi or Christian preacher teach, preach, or simply explain this commandment? Before nodding our heads in agreement with the rabbi or saying amen to the preacher, we need to understand *two* Hebrew words. They are the English words *take* and *vain,* which in Hebrew are נשא (*nasa*) and שוא (*shav*). Let's get to work.

First we must understand the meaning of the phrase "taking the name." In biblical Hebrew, to *take* words means to speak them. Please *take* the time to open your Bible and *take* a look at the following examples. If you noticed, I just used the English word *take* twice, but neither has the same meaning as *take* in Hebrew. The following prophecies of Balaam illustrate the way that *"take"* in the Third Commandment is meant to be understood:

> And he took up his parable, and said . . .
> NUMBERS 23:7; 24:3; 24:15

As you can see, to take up a parable means to speak it. Also, you can see the same word used in the context of taking up a lamentation or dirge:

> Hear this word which I take up for you as a dirge, O house of Israel.
> AMOS 5:1

The Hebrew word translated *take up* is נשא (*nasa*). In Hebrew "to take a name" is to lift it up in speech. A great way to remember this word is to think of the NASA space agency that *lifts up* rockets that *take off* from earth.

The word שוא (*shav*), which is translated as *vain,* is a little more complicated, but worth the effort. The problem is that the

English word *vain* does not have a parallel image that matches the interpretation. It is easy to confuse people when the words don't have concrete pictures that you can attach to the meaning. The only image I have of the word *vain* is the junior high school girl who is so beautiful, but so vain. There is an old song that matches this image and goes something like this: *"You're so vain, you probably think this song is about you. You're so vain."* Is this the meaning of taking the name in vain? Is the name like the girl that I should not *take* because she is so vain?

The English translators apparently had a similar problem with this word. They just could not make up their minds about which English word to use when they saw the Hebrew word שוא (*shav*). In fact, there are 12 different words used in our English Bibles for the Hebrew שוא (*shav*): deceit, deceitful, deception, emptiness, empty, false, falsehood, lies, vain, vanity, visions, and worthless. This useful information will help us arrive at our final interpretation of this verse.

As a starting point let's look at the traditional Jewish interpretation of this Hebrew word שוא (*shav*). It seems to be understood as *without good reason,* which is why this commandment is used to reinforce the ban of the name. This is the explanation offered in the Stone Edition Chumash,[92] which provides commentary on every verse in the Torah, including Exodus 20:7:

> It is forbidden to show contempt for God by making an idol, so it is forbidden to disgrace His Name by using it for no valid purpose. The plain meaning of the verse implies that it is forbidden even to utter God's Name casually, for no valid purpose (Ramban).

As I mentioned previously, the Hebrew word in the Third

---

[92] The Stone Edition Chumash, edited by Rabbi Nosson Scherman/Rabbi Meir Zlotowitz. Brooklyn, New York: Mesorah Publications, 2001, page 409.

Commandment translated as *vain* is שוא (*shav*). It has been used to "shove" us around regarding the ban on speaking the name. Did you catch that? To be honest, there is biblical evidence showing that שוא (*shav*) can mean *vain* in the sense of *without purpose*. An example can be found in the book of Jeremiah:

> In vain [*shav*] I have struck your sons, they accepted
> no chastening.
>
> JEREMIAH 2:30

However, when you add the concept of *speaking* "in vain," as is the case with the Third Commandment in Exodus 20:7, the word takes on a different and revelatory meaning! To speak שוא (*shav*) means to speak falsehood or lies, as in the following examples:

> Whose mouths speak deceit [*shav*], and whose right
> hand is a right hand of falsehood [*shaker*].
>
> PSALMS 144:8

This verse contains what is called parallelism, with the two phrases expressing the same basic thought in different words. Deceit (*shav*) and falsehood (*shaker*) are two ways of saying the same thing. There is another verse in this Psalm that uses the same Hebrew word combination:

> Whose mouth speaks deceit [*shav*] and whose right
> hand is a right hand of falsehood [*shaker*].
>
> PSALMS 144:11

What we see is that שוא (*shav*) and שקר (*shaker)* are like dance partners in the Hebrew Scriptures. If we can find an example of *shaker* being used in the place of *shav* or vice versa, then the interpretation party is really on. Strike up the band and get ready to dance! The Ninth Commandment is calling you to the dance floor.

You shall not bear false [שֶׁקֶר, *shaker*] witness against your neighbor.

EXODUS 20:16

When Moses reiterated the Ten Commandments in Deuteronomy, what word do you suppose he used for *false* in this parallel account? In your English Bible you will probably see:

You shall not bear false witness against your neighbor.

DEUTERONOMY 5:20

But if you were to read my Hebrew "left-handed version" you would see this:

Do not testify against your fellow as a vain [שָׁוְא, *shav*] witness.

DEUTERONOMY 5:20 (Keith Johnson Version)

Did you catch that slight difference in my version? When Moses wrote this verse he used שָׁוְא (*shav*) interchangeably with שֶׁקֶר (*shaker*) when speaking of a *false witness*. This is very revealing because it shows us that there is a relationship between the difficult-to-translate word שָׁוְא (*shav*) and the much easier word to translate שֶׁקֶר (*shaker*). This is one of the keys to understanding the Third Commandment about *"taking the name in vain."*

Before we move on to apply this information there is one more verse that will help seal the deal on understanding the Third Commandment. As a reminder, we now know that to *take* the name means to *speak* it. When we add *vain* in this context it means to speak falsely. Now open your Bible to the following verse:

You shall not bear [נָשָׂא, *nasa*] a false [שָׁוְא, *shav*] report; do not join your hand with a wicked man to be a malicious witness.

EXODUS 23:1

This commandment uses both the verb נשא (*nasa*) for *bear* and the adjective שוא (*shav*) for *false*. This is almost identical to the Third Commandment. The only difference is that one prohibits speaking the name (שם, *shem*) falsely while the other prohibits speaking a false report (שמע, *shema*). Notice that many English translators render the word *shav* as *false* in Exodus 23:1 and Deuteronomy 5:20, but translate the same word as *in vain* in Exodus 20:7 and Deuteronomy 5:11, even though all four passages deal with vain/false speech.[93] Look them up for yourself.

Exodus 23:1 confirms, by *two* witnesses in Scripture, that to be a "vain witness" means to be a "false witness," because to speak vanity means to speak falsehood.[94]

Now that we have the explanation of the commandment, we can move on to the application of this first "fire-fueling" verse. *"What does it mean to speak falsely?"* In biblical times people made oaths by swearing in the name of a god or a king. So to understand how to swear or make an oath we must look at the formulation of ancient vows. A vow consisted of an individual saying, "As X lives" (X being the name of a god or king) followed by a statement of what was being promised or declared.[95] We see such a vow made by Joseph *in the name of Pharaoh* when he promised his brothers:

> By this you will be tested: by the life of Pharaoh, you shall not go from this place unless your youngest brother comes here!
>
> GENESIS 42:15

Joseph was swearing by the authority of the king of Egypt. In the Tanach there are 35 times where this exact form of swearing is used in reference to יהוה. Here are *two* examples of individuals swearing by His authority:

---

[93] RSV, NIV, and NSRV replace *in vain* with *misuse,* although they still translate the other verses as *false.*

[94] Nehemia Gordon, "The Pronunciation of the Name," www.Karaite-Korner.org.

[95] Nehemia Gordon, "The Pronunciation of the Name," www.Karaite-Korner.org.

Saul vowed to her by יהוה, saying, "As יהוה lives, no punishment will come upon you for this thing."

1 SAMUEL 28:10

And you will swear, 'As יהוה lives,' in truth, in justice and in righteousness . . .

JEREMIAH 4:2

Even יהוה uses the same words to make a vow on His own existence. The following *two* examples are very enlightening:

"As I live," declares יהוה . . .

JEREMIAH 22:24

Indeed, I lift up My hand to heaven, and say, as I live forever.

DEUTERONOMY 32:40

To swear or make a vow is a very serious act. There are four times in the Hebrew Scriptures where יהוה swears by Himself![96] In each case He uses the Hebrew phrase *"In Me I swear,"* whereas the English says *"I swear by Myself."* You might also find it interesting to consider where the courts got the idea to "raise your right hand and swear" before testifying. It clearly reflects the biblical practice of taking oaths.

In English you will see many examples of יהוה saying *"I swore."* The *two* words in Hebrew that are translated into English as *"I swore"* are very informative in helping us understand the Third Commandment. The *two* words are נשא (*nasa*) *to take up* and יד (*yad*) *hand.* Let's notice two examples:

I will bring you to the land which I swore to give to Abraham. . . .

EXODUS 6:8

---

[96] See Genesis 22:16, Isaiah 45:23, Jeremiah 22:5, Jeremiah 49:13.

Also I swore to them in the wilderness that I would scatter them. . . .

EZEKIEL 20:23

What יהוה is saying in Hebrew means *"I lifted my hand."* Do you understand where we are going with this yet? The following passage shows us another way that vows were made:

Who may ascend into the hill of יהוה? And who may stand in His holy place? He who has clean hands and a pure heart, who has not lifted up his soul to falsehood and has not sworn deceitfully.

PSALMS 24:3–4

This verse might be one you just quickly read and leave the understanding to someone else. That would really be unfortunate, because you would miss the dance that is coming. In biblical times a person making a vow often swore by someone's "soul." We see this when both Abigail and Uriah swore by David's life/soul and Abigail also swore by יהוה:

Now therefore, my lord, as יהוה lives, and as your soul lives . . .

1 SAMUEL 25:26

By your life and the life of your soul, I will not do this thing.

2 SAMUEL 11:11

Let's review the last part of Psalms 24:4. This is what it says in the Keith Johnson Version based on the Hebrew Scriptures.

Who has not lifted [נשא, *nasa*] <u>My</u> <u>soul</u> in vain [שוא, *shav*] and has not sworn deceitfully.

PSALMS 24:4 (Keith Johnson Version)

Thus to *"take my soul in vain"* means to make a false vow by someone's soul! Here is a great opportunity to check my version against two other English versions. Many English Bibles incorrectly translate the Hebrew word נַפְשִׁי (*nafshi*), which means *my soul,* as *his soul* (see BHS and note).[97] This little exercise was for you "Bereans"[98] who are checking to see if what I am saying is in the Scriptures.

This verse also shows us that taking a soul in vain (i.e., vowing falsely) is equivalent to swearing deceitfully. Now you be the rabbi or the preacher and tell the world what the Third Commandment means so that they can nod their head, shout amen, and join the dance!

To take the name יהוה in vain means to lift up His name with a vow that comes out of your mouth even though you have deceit in your heart! You can swear to a god if you want to and take your chances. Just don't ever include the name יהוה in a false or deceptive vow! Now compare your English Bible with my translation of the Third Commandment:

> You shall not lift up the name יהוה your Elohim in a vow as a lie, because יהוה shall not leave unpunished anyone who makes a false vow in His name.
>
> EXODUS 20:7 (Keith Johnson Version)

I now know where the "vows" of my boyhood friends came from when they would say "I swear on my mother's grave/soul" or "I swear to God." I am glad they never swore by the name יהוה!

Before you think that I am claiming some new and revelatory interpretation of this verse you should know that this interpretation has existed for a very long time. In fact, Nehemia and I, in our book *A Prayer to Our Father: Hebrew Origins of the Lord's*

---

[97] BHS stands for *Biblia Hebraica Stuttgartensia* (edited by K. Elliger and W. Rudolph, et al, Deutsche Bibelgesellschaft Stuttgart, 1967/77, 1983). To date BHS is the most precise printing of the Hebrew Scriptures, only rarely deviating from the Leningrad Codex.
[98] Acts 17:11.

Prayer, give four examples of both ancient and modern interpretations that confirm what I have presented here.[99] The truth is that the oldest known interpretations of this verse by the *Targum Onkelos,* the official catechism of the Catholic Church, Protestant reformers, and modern Jewish translators all agree that this commandment is forbidding false oaths. They just choose to tell you that it means the name should not be spoken.

If I have not convinced you with this detailed study and you still need more biblical examples that shed light on the Third Commandment, here is another one to consider:

> You shall not swear falsely by My name, so as to profane the name of your Elohim; I am יהוה.
>
> LEVITICUS 19:12

Many readers may be surprised to learn that we are actually *commanded* twice in the book of Deuteronomy to swear by the name יהוה.

> You shall fear only יהוה your Elohim; and you shall worship Him and swear by His name.
>
> DEUTERONOMY 6:13

> You shall fear יהוה your Elohim; you shall serve Him and cling to Him, and you shall swear by His name.
>
> DEUTERONOMY 10:20

I have one simple question about these two almost identical verses. How can I swear (make an oath) by the name יהוה if I am prohibited from pronouncing His name?

The prophet Jeremiah takes this one step further and invites Gentiles to learn from Israel how to swear by the name יהוה:

---

[99] Gordon, N. and Johnson, K. *A Prayer to Our Father: Hebrew Origins of The Lord's Prayer.* Hilkiah Press, 2009, pages 104-105.

Then if they will really learn the ways of My people, to swear by My name, "As יהוה lives," even as they taught My people to swear by Baal [Lord], they will be built up in the midst of My people.

JEREMIAH 12:16

If we can overcome our fear of the ban on the name and learn to swear by the name יהוה, we can become a built-up people in the midst of Israel. You might want to reread this section before moving on. Take some time to reflect on why so much effort has been expended to keep us from seeing and knowing the name יהוה.

The second *fire-fueling* passage may not be as well known as the Third Commandment, but the interpretation and application have reached beyond the walls of synagogues and churches. This passage must be examined according to what I consider the most underused concept in the study of Scripture: *context*. I am convinced that if more people looked at context we would have a lot less fighting and confusion in churches and synagogues today. How many different religious groups base their doctrines on just one verse of the Bible without looking at "the whole counsel of Scripture?" This is the case with the following well-known verse:

Moreover, the one who blasphemes the name יהוה shall surely be put to death; all the congregation shall certainly stone him. The alien as well as the native, when he blasphemes the Name, shall be put to death.

LEVITICUS 24:16

Many people who have read, quoted, preached, and written about this verse may be picking out the stones they would like to throw at me. If you are one of these stone-throwers, please allow me the opportunity to make an important point before you take aim.

Remember, context is the key to this passage. If we only had this one verse, it would be much more difficult to understand. The Hebrew word נקב (*naqav*), whose basic meaning is *designate, bore a hole, or pierce*, is used 19 times in the Tanach. The English translators liked the word "blaspheme." In fact, they liked it so much that they used it in various forms 45 times. Of course, they had to use three different Hebrew words to have that many occurrences. I guess "blaspheme" is a word invented for the sound effect.

As you may know, some Bible commentators argue that this verse proves that the personal name of our Heavenly Father must not be spoken. In fact, this is one of those "proof text" arguments used by some to perpetuate the ban on the name. We must read seven verses to set the context:

> Now the son of an Israelite woman, whose father was Egyptian, went out among the sons of Israel; and the Israelite woman's son and a man of Israel struggled with each other in the camp. The son of the Israelite woman blasphemed the Name and cursed. So they brought him to Moses. . . . They put him in custody so that the command of יהוה might be made clear to them. Then יהוה spoke to Moses, saying, "Bring the one who has cursed outside the camp, and let all who heard him lay their hands on his head; then let all the congregation stone him. You shall speak to the sons of Israel, saying, 'If anyone curses his God, then he will bear his sin. Moreover, the one who blasphemes the name יהוה shall surely be put to death; all the congregation shall stone him. The alien as well as the native, when he blasphemes the Name, shall be put to death.'"
>
> LEVITICUS 24:10–16

Now we can analyze the verse in its context. Notice that even Moses did not know what the "command of יהוה" would be for this offense. This took place after the giving of the Ten Commandments, so it did not involve the breaking of the Third Commandment, *"taking the name in vain."* Moses knew that he was not qualified to make a decision about this complicated and serious matter, so he called upon the One called אלהים שפטים בארץ (Elohim Who Judges in the Earth)[100] to render His judgment.

The sentence for this crime was that the son of the Israelite woman should be executed. Then יהוה defined under what circumstances a person would receive this punishment. The key is that a person would have to specifically "blaspheme" the Name יהוה and curse. This is the connection between blasphemy and cursing. Usually an expert curser can נקב (*naqav*) *pierce* your ears with his words.

The many people who demand that their god should *"damn"* something are not cursing their god. If you curse the holy personal name יהוה, then according to the biblical standard death is required! As you can see, יהוה takes His name very seriously.

The following two translations of Leviticus 24 really troubled me as I wrote this study.

> If he also pronounces the name LORD, he shall be put to death. . . . if he has thus pronounced the Name, he shall be put to death.
> LEVITICUS 24:16 (Jewish Publication Society)

When I saw the above translation my heart became heavy. I felt even worse when one of my study partners brought the Septuagint version of this verse to my attention:

> The one who names the name LORD shall be put to death. . . . when he names the name of the LORD he shall be put to death.
> LEVITICUS 24:16 (Greek Septuagint)[101]

These two translations threw me off course. I needed to consult my Hebrew teacher and scholar Nehemia Gordon:

---

[100] Elohim Shophtim Ba'aretz, Psalms 58:11 in English and 58:12 in the Hebrew Scriptures.
[101] Translation by Keith Johnson from the Greek Septuagint LXX 1.

The JPS and Septuagint translations are correct, as *nokev* really does mean to specify a name (as in Numbers 1:17). The context in verse 15 is cursing and verse 16 adds that when someone pronounces the name (as part of such a curse) he is to be put to death. Notice that the JPS has "also"; that is, he curses and *also* pronounces the name (as part of the curse). The Greek text literally uses the root word "also" as a translation of "name" for the Hebrew vav at the beginning of the verse, which is a vav of contrast, i.e., "but if he pronounces the name" (as part of the curse).[102]

Once again, context comes to the rescue! Leviticus 24:15 makes it clear:

You shall speak to the sons of Israel, saying, 'If anyone curses his God, then he will bear his sin.

One of the many things I have learned from Nehemia over the years is to check things out for myself. Hopefully you are like me and you want access to information so that rather than being told to toe the party line, you can make your own informed decisions.

Our Heavenly Father יהוה expects us to vow in His name truthfully and to never blaspheme or curse His name under any circumstance. It is a tremendous privilege to know His name and use it to His glory! You now have proof that the traditional ban on saying the Holy Name is not biblical. In fact, it is not even responsible. You also know that there were agendas being pushed in the process of translating this name. This tradition must be changed! The ban must be lifted!

I wish this tradition and translation confusion that keeps people from speaking the name could be explained away as ancient

---

[102] Nehemia Gordon in consultation with Keith Johnson.

history, far removed from present-day practice. But it seems that the spirit of the second-century ban on the name lives on today among Jewish authorities, Protestant translators, and Catholic leaders. I can hear ancient voices saying, *"You don't need to know it; it is too complicated and it is beyond your understanding."* I disagree, and I hope you do too. Unfortunately, I also hear present-day voices that want to prohibit us from receiving the blessings that are linked to proclaiming the name. It seems that history is being repeated.

Warning:

Before we venture into the next four chapters, I am compelled to warn you that if you apply the information that you are learning you will be going against the modern-day ban on the pronunciation of the name of our Heavenly Father. In the summer of 2008 the Pope directed that the following letter be sent to the Bishops of the Catholic Church under the title, *"Letter to the Bishops' Conferences on The Name of God."* Here it is for your review:

> By directive of the Holy Father, in accord with the Congregation for the Doctrine of the Faith, this Congregation for Divine Worship and the Discipline of the Sacraments deems it convenient to communicate to the Bishops' Conference in regards to the translation and pronunciation, in a liturgical setting of the Divine Name signified in the sacred *tetragrammaton,* along with a number of directives. . . .

> As regards the sacred name of God itself, translators must use the greatest faithfulness and respect. In particular as the Instruction *Liturgium authenticam* (n. 41 states) : In accordance with immemorial tradition, which in deed is already evident in the above-

mentioned "Septuagint" version, the name of Almighty God expressed by the Hebrew *tetragrammaton* and rendered in Latin by the word *Dominus,* is to be rendered into any given vernacular by a word equivalent in meaning.

Notwithstanding such a clear norm, in recent years the practice has crept in of pronouncing the God of Israel's proper name, known as the holy or divine *tetragrammaton,* written with four consonants of the Hebrew alphabet in the form of יהוה. . . . It is therefore our intention with the present Letter, to set out some essential facts which lie behind the above-mentioned norm and to establish some directives to be observed in this matter.

The letter goes on to "establish the following facts" that:

- Since the name is unpronounceable it was replaced with *"Adonai which means LORD."*
- The Greek translation rendered the Hebrew *tetragram-maton* with the Greek word *"Kyrios which means LORD."*
- The title (Lord) is interchangeable between the God of Israel and Messiah of the Christian faith, even though it is not in fact used for the Messiah of Israel.
- First generation Greek-speaking Christians *"never pro-nounced the divine tetragrammaton."*
- In order to stay faithful to Church tradition from the beginning, *"the tetragrammaton was never pronounced in the Christian context or ever translated into any of the languages into which the Bible was translated."*

In light of these facts, the following "directives" are to be observed:

1. In liturgical celebrations, in songs and prayers the name of God in the form of the *tetragrammaton* YHWH is neither to be used or pronounced.

2. For the translation of the Biblical text in modern languages, destined for the liturgical usage of the Church, what is already prescribed by n. 41 of the Instruction of *Liturgium authenticam* is to be followed; that is, the divine *tetragrammaton* is to be rendered by the equivalent of *Adonai/Kurio,* "Lord," "Signore," "Seigneur," "Herr," etc.

3. In translating, in the liturgical context, texts in which are present, one after the other, either the Hebrew term *Adonai* or the *tetragrammaton* YHWH, Adonai is to be translated "Lord" and the form "God" is to be used for the *tetragrammaton* YHWH, similar to what happens in the Greek translation of the Septuagint and in the Latin translation of the Vulgate.

From the Congregation for Divine Worship and the Discipline of the Sacraments, 29 June 2008.[103]

Facts versus Fiction

Since the aforementioned *"five facts"* are the basis of the modern-day ban on the name, it only makes sense that I at least give an abbreviated response. The *fiction* statements are direct quotes from the papal letter; the *facts* are my abbreviated responses.

1. Fiction: *Since the name is unpronounceable it was replaced with Adonai which means LORD.*

   Fact: Actually the name is not unpronounceable. Rather, it is prohibited from being pronounced by rabbinic authority,

---

[103] The full text of the letter is available on the USCCB website: http://www.usccb.org/liturgy/NameOfGod.pdf. Still have questions? Contact CUF's Catholic Responses department: questions@cuf.org.

which has been perpetuated by both Catholic and Protestant translators. The meaning of *Adonai* is "lord" or "master," not LORD (capitalized to represent the name of God), as claimed by English translators.

2. Fiction: *The Greek translation rendered the Hebrew tetra-grammaton with the Greek word "Kyrios" which means LORD.*

   Fact: The Greek word *Kyrios* has the exact same meaning as the Hebrew word *Adonai* which is "lord" or "master." *Kyrios* has no intrinsic meaning that makes it worthy of divine status. It is simply a title that is being substituted for the name. There is also manuscript evidence that the early versions of the Septuagint actually included the name in Paleo-Hebrew letters.[104]

3. Fiction: *The title (Lord) is interchangeable between the God of Israel and Messiah of the Christian faith, even though it is not in fact used for the Messiah of Israel.*

   Fact: There is no precedent in the Hebrew Bible for the name behind the title (LORD) being interchangeable between the God of Israel and the Messiah of the Christian faith. This is an example of theology taking precedent over textual, linguistic, and translation integrity.

4. Fiction: *First generation Greek-speaking Christians never pronounced the divine tetragrammaton.*

   Fact: This is a gratuitous assertion. There is no evidence to support this claim.

---

[104] This can be seen in some Dead Sea Scroll papyri and early versions of the Greek Septuagint.

5. Fiction: *The tetragrammaton was never pronounced in the Christian context or ever translated into any of the languages into which the Bible was translated.*

Fact: The Hebrew Scrolls were considered the "Scriptures" and "the Oracles of God" by *Jesus* and every writer of the New Testament. This name was read and spoken by pockets of Jews and Christians until at least 70 C.E. before it was banned by governmental and religious authorities. There is also proof that the name was transliterated into other languages of the Bible, including English!

When I first became aware of this letter from the Vatican, I was still debating with myself about making this information about the name יהוה public. This letter ended the debate and sealed the deal. If the Catholic authorities felt confident enough to prohibit the name from being spoken based on tradition, I certainly have even more confidence to proclaim the name based on biblical truth. In fact, I am grateful that the Pope spurred me on to achieve my purpose. Every opportunity that I am given, I will stand against this ban! Any individual, church, or organization that uses its "authority" to ban the use of the name יהוה is teaching people something that is in direct conflict with the Holy Scriptures. This should not be! The ban must be broken!

My response is clear and simple to this *"directive"* from the Pope and his committee. It is unacceptable for organized religion to obstruct our access to an intimate relationship with our real Holy Heavenly Father!

I experienced the effects of this ban while attending my son Kyle's football game at Clemson University in South Carolina. Being originally from Minnesota, it has been a pleasant surprise to hear public prayers before football games down here in the South. I have heard a variety of religious leaders from diverse religious backgrounds lead this pre-game prayer ritual and it has been quite refreshing.

During one of these pre-game events the prayer was being lead by a representative of the Catholic student organization. He began by naming a man who had just died. At first I thought he was praising the man. Then I thought he was just addressing the crowd. By the time I realized he was praying he was almost done. In fact, he spoke this dead man's name three times along with the wish *"may we be just like him."* If he had not said *"amen,"* I would not have known that he was praying at all. Let it suffice to say he took the ban on the name to its logical conclusion. There was no sense of intimacy or personal connection to יהוה at all in his prayer. I wondered how the real Holy Father in heaven viewed this "prayer." Interestingly enough, there were *two* lightning delays at this game which caused the teams to leave the field *twice.* These two lightning strikes delayed the game for over an hour and it became the longest game in Clemson football history. Okay, so it was an interesting coincidence. Do you mind a little Scripture to go along with the coincidence?

> Then יהוה will appear over them, and His arrow will go forth like lightning; and Adonai יהוה will blow the trumpet, and will march in the storm winds of the south.
>
> ZECHARIAH 9:14

The Pope and his committee, through their directives, are keeping people from having the intimate relationship with our Father that comes by praying, singing, pronouncing, vowing in, greeting, writing, or sanctifying the personal and intimate name יהוה. In a way it feels like church history is repeating itself. However, this time we have access to a wealth of information that can give us confidence to know our Heavenly Father and call Him by His name. What will you do? It is decision time. Either you can put this book down and submit to the ban, or you can continue this journey with me and receive a great blessing!

This chapter was as challenging for me to write as I am sure it has been for some people to read. I sometimes get frustrated thinking about what has been done to the one name that is absolutely necessary for our understanding of Scripture and our comprehension of the essence and character of our Heavenly Father.

I have decided to channel my frustration into positive energy and use it to present this information and proclaim His name. The time has come to take back our Heavenly Father's name so we can begin to worship Him the way He desires.

Are you willing to seek the truth about this name that has been hidden for so long? Are you ready for the game of hide-and-seek to end? When I was a boy I used to love to play hide-and-seek. I could find such great places to hide that no one could find me for hours. I could hardly wait to hear the high-pitched voices of my frustrated friends shout, *"Alley Alley in come free!"* In some neighborhoods they would yell, *"Come out, come out, wherever you are!"* The joy and satisfaction of winning the game were exhilarating when I finally showed myself to my defeated friends.

If you are tired of the game of hide-and-seek that we have been forced to play because of the agenda of men, then shout right now at your English Bible, *"Alley Alley in come free!"* Yell at the top of your voice to the information in the Hebrew Bible, *"Come out, come out, wherever you are!"* These are the words that I want to ring out everywhere, from the Western Wall in Jerusalem to the Crystal Cathedral in California. I want these words to cause the Pope in Rome and the preacher in Harlem to agree that this name must be revealed! The name יהוה is ready to come out and claim victory.

He is called אל מסתתר (El Who Hides Himself)[105] and He is the one who allowed His name to be hidden. The good news is that the time has come for His name to be revealed again!

> "I have not spoken in secret, from somewhere in a
> land of darkness; I have not said to Jacob's

---

[105] El Mistatear, Isaiah 45:15.

descendants, 'Seek me in vain.' I, יהוה, speak the truth; I declare what is right."

ISAIAH 45:19

If you are ready to meet and greet the winner of the tradition, translation, and theological game of hide-and-seek that has been going on for the last 1,900 years, then shout Amen! Amen! After you finish shouting, keep reading!

וְאָמְרוּ לִי מַה שְּׁמוֹ מָה אֹמַר אֲלֵהֶם

And they will say to me, 'What is His name?' What should I say to them?

EXODUS 3:13

ז

ZAYIN

CHAPTER SEVEN

THE ULTIMATE QUESTION

Zeal for knowledge and understanding usually means that you must be willing to ask questions and diligently search for answers. When it came time for Moses to lead the children of Israel out of Egypt, he realized he needed the answer to one final question. Even today, in spite of the impediments of *tradition and translation,* both Jewish and Christian seekers of truth are asking this same question. Let's look at the passage that leads up to this ultimate question in preparation for Israel's deliverance from Egypt.

> Now Moses was pasturing the flock of Jethro his father-in-law, the priest of Midian; and he led the flock to the west side of the wilderness and came to Horeb, the mountain of Elohim. And the angel of יהוה appeared to him in a blazing fire from the midst of a bush; and he looked, and behold, the bush was burning with fire, yet the bush was not consumed. So Moses said, "I must turn aside now and see this marvelous sight, why the bush is not burned up."
>
> EXODUS 3:1–2

Please stop and look at this *marvelous sight.* I am convinced that if you take the time to *turn aside and look,* you will see something that deserves your full attention. The first thing to notice is a bush burning in the desert; it might catch your attention, but would not necessarily be considered *marvelous.* Sometimes during a storm a lightning strike can cause a tree or bush to catch on fire. However, if the bush was in the arid desert and continued burning unabated, it certainly would catch the attention of an experienced shepherd like Moses.

This fire is not doing what it is supposed to do, which is to consume the fuel and burn itself out. Three elements must be present for a fire to occur: a spark (heat), fuel, and oxygen. If any of the three is lacking, there can be no fire. This is why firefighters use water to extinguish fires; it reduces the heat. Moses knew that this was no ordinary fire so he slowed down and turned aside to *see this marvelous sight.*

At this point I am stuck if I only have my English Bible and, like Moses, really want to see *why the bush is not burned up.* I might be able to guess that, even though there is a *blazing fire,* the presence of the angel of יהוה makes the properties of the fire function differently. However, my Bible does not say that, so I am still guessing what makes this fire *marvelous.* It does not say that Moses turned aside because he saw the angel of יהוה in the fire. My Bible clearly states that he saw a bush *burning with fire, yet the bush was not consumed.* There are no further clues to help me figure out what is happening here. Let's go on a journey of discovery and take a look at the Hebrew text to see if we can learn anything more about this extraordinary fire.

First of all, I am suspicious of the English words *blazing fire.* Sure enough, the Hebrew word בלבת (*b'labat,* blazing) is very rare. There are only *two* places in the entire Tanach where the word is used in this form; the other time it is translated as *heart,* in the feminine singular construct form, which is the same form that appears here.[106] The English word *heart* usually comes from the Hebrew לבב (*levav*), which is a masculine noun, rather than the feminine noun we see in this passage. The only difference between the two occurrences of בלבת (*b'labat*) is that the *heart* form has a suffix while the *blazing* form has a preposition. The key to the translation and interpretation of this unique word is the preposition that is used as the first letter, which is a ב (*bet*). This one letter gives us a huge clue.

There is a technical term that is used for this preposition that should make us slow down even further. The term is *Bet essentiae*, which conveys the idea of *manifesting as or like*.[107] The same grammatical phenomenon occurs in Exodus 6:3, where most English translations convey the following: *"I appeared as/like El Shaddai."* This literally means that יהוה manifested like *El of my breasts* or *mighty breasts*. This is probably a little controversial for the average English Bible reader, but for the Hebrew reader it is a picture of strength and power combined with nurture and protection. No Hebrew reader would think this was a literal picture of El with breasts. Our verse in Exodus 3 could have been translated, *"The angel of יהוה appeared as or like a blazing* fire in the midst of the bush." This translation helps us understand that what Moses saw was *"like a blazing fire,"* but not necessarily a literal, functioning common fire.

The next thing I want to know is what the original Hebrew word is for this *bush* that doesn't burn. The English words *bush* or *bushes* are used 18 times in the Old Testament and are derived from seven different Hebrew words, so when we see one of these English words it could be based on any one of the seven Hebrew words. They are: שיח, קוץ, סיר, ערוער, סנה, נעצוץ, חוח (*sheach, qots, sir, aroer, seneh, na'tsuts,* and *choach*). The Hebrew word סנה (*seneh*) is very rare. In fact, Moses is the only author in the entire

---

[106] See Ezekiel 16:30 where the form לבתך is used with the second person singular suffix (your heart).
[107] Kautzsch E. and Cowley A. E. *Gesenius' Hebrew Grammar.* Oxford University Press, second edition, 1988, paragraph 119, page 379, section i.

Tanach who uses it. Moses uses סנה (*seneh*) six times; five of the occurrences are right here in the *burning bush* passage. The sixth time he uses the word is very enlightening, but before I mention that verse I want to better understand the meaning of this word for bush.

The word סנה (*seneh*) here seems to convey the idea of something like a mulberry bush, possibly with fruit on it. If it had been a tumbleweed bush or a regular thorn bush the color might not stand out. The passage also contains the English word *"behold."* The Hebrew word is הנה (*hineh*), which conveys the idea of something more than a glance. Imagine Moses raising his eyebrows, dropping his staff, and saying, *"Wow!"* Imagine a large fruit bush that appears to be burning but produces no smoke, combined with the spectrum of light from the fire and the color of the fruit as a background. Is it possible that Moses saw an amazingly colorful spectrum of light in the dry, dusty desert? Clearly something is different about the סנה (*seneh*) bush. What Moses saw caused him to הנה (*hineh*) *behold* this marvelous sight.

The sixth and final use of the word סנה (*seneh*) was when Moses pronounced a blessing over Joseph. This verse adds further illumination to the *bush* that doesn't burn:

> And with the choice things of the earth and its fullness, and the favor of Him who dwelt [שכן, *shaken*] in the bush [סנה, *seneh*] . . .
>
> DEUTERONOMY 33:16

This *bush* is reserved for favor from the presence of the One who lives in heaven, but sometimes chooses to dwell (שכן, *shaken*) in a bush that looks like a flame of fire on earth. שכן (*shaken*) is the root of the word for the tabernacle (משכן, *mishkan*), where the glory dwelt (Psalms 26:8).

When you combine something that looks like fire with a large fruit bush that displays His glorious presence, it requires a second look. You have to slow down, turn aside, see, and behold this *marvelous sight!* Maybe our process of discovery will also attract the attention of Elohim so He will call to us from the סנה (*seneh*) bush.

> When יהוה saw that he turned aside to look, Elohim called to him from the midst of the bush [*seneh*] and said, "Moses, Moses!" And he said, "Here I am."
>
> EXODUS 3:4

Are you still with me? When יהוה had Moses' full attention, He did *two* things. First, he called his name twice, *"Moses, Moses!"* I have already explained my opinion about why things happen in *twos*. I am sure Moses would have only needed one holy call of his name from Elohim to realize who was calling. There must be some significance for there to be *two* calls. Until I hear otherwise, I am taking the position that the first call is for heaven and the second call is for earth as a *witness* that something crucial has happened or is about to happen.

The second thing יהוה did was to command Moses to *take off his sandals because the place he was standing was holy ground.*[108] Moses was close enough to the bush to be on holy ground, yet he apparently felt no physical discomfort. Was that because the bush was not literally on fire and, therefore, emitting no heat?

At this point I would like you to consider doing something as a sign of acknowledgement of where we are in this process of discovery. Would you be willing to do the same thing יהוה asked Moses to do and remove the barrier between you and this holy ground? Seriously, would you stop reading and take off your shoes, slippers, boots, or sandals out of respect for this holy moment?

We are about to interact with the holiest name in the universe. Maybe this is a good time to reflect and possibly adjust our attitudes and actions for the remainder of this study. Are you willing to be like Moses and slow down, turn aside, and remove your shoes, or are you like a lot of people who just ignore the signs and hurry along, maintaining the status quo? I hope you will not

---

[108] Exodus 3:5.

miss this special opportunity to interact with the light of His word from this *fire*.

There is a theme that runs through Scripture regarding fire and light. These *two* phenomena seem to get the attention of people like nothing else on earth. Both fire and light have been used in religions around the world to simulate the presence of the Divine.

Fire has been used to shape the entire industrialized world. It is fire that extracts copper from rock, makes glass out of sand, and turns iron and coal into steel. Fire allows cars to move and airplanes to fly. Man uses wood, coal, gasoline, and other fuels to make fire. He has also tapped into the power of the atom. What is even more fascinating is that יהוה has manifested Himself in this same powerful picture of fire throughout the pages of Scripture. I encourage you to take some time to research the many ways that the presence of יהוה is connected to fire. You might be motivated to write your own study about this amazing phenomenon. One thing I hope you find in your study is that יהוה sometimes answers by fire!

> Then you call on the name of your Elohim, and I will call on the name יהוה, and the Elohim who answers by fire, He is Elohim.
>
> 1 KINGS 18:24

> And [David] called to יהוה and He answered him with fire from heaven on the altar of burnt offering.
>
> 1 CHRONICLES 21:26

The subject of light is even more amazing! In fact, I would argue that light is one of the most important manifestations of יהוה that ever was or ever will be. I would go so far as to say that even though light was created, it is also a part of the very essence of our Creator! In other words, light came from יהוה just like woman came from man. It is an inherent property that has been manifested and given to us to reveal one aspect of His essence.

I would like to briefly comment about the speed of light. Visible light travels at 186,000 miles per second—the equivalent of seven times around the earth! In the universe that יהוה created, we just can't measure distance in inches, feet, yards, or even miles. In order to grasp the magnitude of His universe, we must measure in light years. One light year is the distance light travels in a year, which is just less than 6 trillion miles.

A simple example of something that must be measured in light years rather than miles is the distance between earth and the closest star beyond the sun. Our sun is 93 million miles from earth. In order to reach Alpha Centauri, the next closest star, we would need to travel the distance between the earth and the sun 277,000 times. That is a distance of 4.3 light years or more than 25 trillion miles! As you read this book there is a space probe called *Voyager* that is traveling 35,000 miles per hour; it has enough fuel to continue for approximately 8,000 years. In order for that probe to cover the distance from earth to Alpha Centauri, 4.3 light years away, it would need to travel for approximately 80,000 years! Speed is just one of the properties of light. We could also discuss color and its other properties.

It is amazing how many places in Scripture there is a connection between יהוה and light. If you do a study on this subject, you will learn things like the rainbow of light in the sky is a sign of a promise and His word is like a light for guidance on earth. I better not get started. However, there are *two* verses that I must share here.

> Come, house of Jacob, and let us walk by the light of יהוה.
>
> ISAIAH 2:5

> No longer will you have the sun for light by day, nor for brightness will the moon give you light; but you will have יהוה for an everlasting light, and your Elohim for your glory.
>
> ISAIAH 60:19

Maybe now you can understand why I assert that light is part of the very essence of יהוה. Before we return to the main topic of this study, I would like to share just a little more information.

Let's go back to the imaginary meeting in heaven from Chapter Two. Do you remember what I said about the first words recorded in the Hebrew Scriptures, which are directly from the mouth of יהוה and written for all (who are willing to try their left hand) to see? If you open your Hebrew Bible to Genesis 1:3 you will see these words: יהי אור (*Yehee Or*), which are translated as *"Let there be light."* It should not be a surprise that one of the names of our Heavenly Father is יהוה אורי (יהוה My Light).[109]

It is remarkable and creative that the first word spoken, יהי (*Yehee*), is the same Hebrew root word for the name יהוה. Notice that the first *two* letters of יהי match exactly the first *two* letters of the name יהוה. This is not mere coincidence. The Hebrew word translated *"let there be"* and the name of our Heavenly Father יהוה come from the same Hebrew root word היה (*hayah*). This verb היה (*hayah*) is used 3,576 times in the Hebrew Bible! The reason it looks different in this verse is because it is in the jussive,[110] which is why in English we say *"Let there be."* The Hebrew jussive form in this particular verse means "Be!"[111]

When יהוה gave the command to light, there was no delay, debate, discussion, or denial. The Almighty One was commanding the action. That is why the same word combination is used for the result of this command: ויהי אור (*Vayehee Or*) *and light was!* The One who spoke *"Be"* to light is the One who is speaking to you and me! This nugget is for all who are stuck back in Chapter Four ("Above Everything") and who are still wondering if there is a

---

[109] יהוה Oree, Psalms 27:1.

[110] The jussive is used to express all the nuances of will from a superior to an inferior: command, exhortation, advice, invitation, permission. Jouon, Paul, and Muraoka T. *A Grammar of Biblical Hebrew*. Editrice Pontificio Istituto Biblico, Rome, 2000. Page 376, section 114 h.

[111] The jussive can be a commandment just like the imperative. The jussive is יְהִי whereas the imperative is הֱיֵה for masculine (Exodus 18:19) and הֲיִי for feminine (Genesis 24:60).

connection between His name and His word. Maybe this little Hebrew grammar lesson helped.

Now back to Moses and the marvelous sight of light! As you may know, the story in this passage sets the context for the exodus of the people from Egypt. Even though יהוה appeared to Moses, he still had to ask the question that we are asking now:

> Then Moses said to Elohim, "Behold, I am going to the sons of Israel, and I shall say to them, 'The Elohim of your fathers has sent me to you.' Now they may say to me, 'What is His name?' What shall I say to them?" Elohim said to Moses, "I AM WHO I AM;" and he said, "Thus you shall say to the sons of Israel, 'I AM has sent me to you.'" Elohim, furthermore, said to Moses, "Thus you shall say to the sons of Israel, 'יהוה', the Elohim of your fathers, the Elohim of Abraham, the Elohim of Isaac, and the Elohim of Jacob, has sent me to you.' This is My name forever, and this is My memorial-name to all generations."
>
> EXODUS 3:13–15

I have three issues (not two) from this important passage to address about the revelation of the name יהוה. First we have to understand why Moses would ask the question about the name, and then address why יהוה would reveal His name. Finally, we need to learn what the expectations and applications for the use of His name were back then and what they are now.

The Question

Moses spent many years in Egypt. He knew that the gods of Egypt all had names and areas of "authority." There were gods of the water, the animals, the crops, the sun, the moon, and many other things. If you study the plagues that were inflicted upon Egypt you will find that יהוה was showing the Egyptians and the

Israelites that He is the One who is אלהי האלהים ואדני האדנים (Elohim of the gods and Adonim of the lords).[112] He is the one and only Elohim and the false gods of Egypt had no power. Moses knew that the Israelite people had been surrounded by the worship of false deities and that they would expect a name for the One who would deliver them from the hand of Pharaoh. Moses needed to know what to tell these curious people about the One who would be for them אלהי ישראל מושיע (Elohim of Israel a Savior!).[113] He had to ask for a name! Moses also knew that if יהוה gave His name, there would be a message behind the name that could be communicated to the people.

Moses asked יהוה a question that was also asked by at least two other men. In Chapter Three I explained that both Jacob and Manoah tried to get an answer to the same type of question about the name, but did not receive the response they wanted. Moses asked the question in a much more ingenious way when he said, *"Now they may say to me, 'What is His name?' What shall I say to them?"* I consider this to be the most intriguing question asked of יהוה in the pages of the entire Bible.

Before I present my research on the answer, I want to give a simple but profound thought about why the Omnipotent, Omniscient, and Omnipresent Supreme Ruler, Sustainer, Merciful, Loving, Most High, Eternal Creator of the Universe was willing to answer the question of a mere man like Moses with the revelation of His name. He answered because the time had come to reveal the power and purpose of the name יהוה and the people were finally prepared to know Him!

There were a number of things that had to happen in order for this date with destiny to take place. יהוה, the great maestro of the orchestra of human affairs conducted a musical masterpiece for all time. He directed many notes, instruments, and musicians. He used people like Noah, Shem, and Abraham; places like Eden, Mount Ararat, and Egypt; and events like the Creation, the Flood,

---

[112] Elohe Haelohim Ve Adonai Haadonim, Deuteronomy 10:17.
[113] Elohe Yisrael Moshia, Isaiah 45:15.

and famines. In the final analysis, Moses was the right man who asked the right question at the right time. As the saying goes, timing is everything!

The Answer

I consider the answer to this intriguing question the most important and revelatory in all of history! I know that is a huge claim, but I am confident the revelation of this awesome name can back it up. This important and revelatory answer informs us about all of history. You might ask, *"Keith, how can you say all of history?"* I can say it because what is being revealed is all about "His story." When אלהים בשמים (Elohim in the Heavens)[114] chose to reveal to Moses that he is אל צדיק ומושיע (Righteous El and Savior)[115] through the name יהוה, then we have a miracle message in the making. These descriptive Hebrew words, connected with the name יהוה, paint a powerful picture of who He is.

Bear with me as I write the answer to Moses' question and our own—from the mouth of יהוה himself—as it appears in the oldest complete vocalized Hebrew manuscript in the world.[116] Of course, I will explain this answer in English, but there is nothing like seeing the name and pronouncing it the way it was spoken by יהוה and recorded by Moses. To refresh your memory, read Exodus 3:13-15 again. After Moses asked the question, אל העֹנה (El Who Answers)[117] gave his response:

"What shall I say to them?" And יהוה said to Moses: אהיה אשר אהיה ['eheyeh 'asher 'eheyeh].

These three Hebrew words are the source of the age-old debate on the meaning of the name יהוה. For hundreds of years

---

[114] Elohim Bashamayim, Joshua 2:11.
[115] El Tsadiq Umoshia, Isaiah 45:21.
[116] The Leningrad Codex B19A.
[117] El ha'oneh, Genesis 35:3.

people have tried to analyze what is very clear in the Hebrew text. In English it basically means *"I AM WHO I AM."* There have been many theories and wild guesses on the "hidden meaning" of אהיה (*'eheyeh*), which is the first common singular form of the verb היה (*hayah*). Do you remember that this verb is the root of His name? In a simple, yet profound way, יהוה is saying, *"I AM like the verb TO BE."* This verb is used in the past, present, and future tenses. Nothing else in the heavens or on the earth can convey this meaning the way יהוה does, because He can back it up!

There are other biblical accounts that witness to the meaning of אהיה (*'eheyeh*). When Moses tried to make the excuse *"I am not a man of words,"* what did יהוה say? *"I AM with your mouth"* (אהיה, *'eheyeh*). When Moses tried again by saying, *"Please send someone else,"* יהוה said, *"I AM with your mouth and with his [Aaron's] mouth"* (אהיה, *'eheyeh*). When Joshua was about to bring the people of Israel into the Promised Land (Joshua 1:5), what did יהוה say? *"I AM with you"* (אהיה, *'eheyeh*). The emphasis is always on the "I." יהוה is the *"I AM."* This is not merely a name of acclaim but it is also a name packed with action.

Since this chapter deals with the ultimate question, let's take this a step further. Imagine with me that an ancient Israelite journalist living in Egypt has been assigned to interview Moses, the *deliverer of the Israelite people.* I am sure he would want to ask Aaron about scheduling an exclusive interview with Moses since he had announced to the elders of Israel that יהוה *"was concerned about them and had seen their misery."*[118] After their worship service, photographs, autographs, and congratulatory pats on the back by the excited Israelites, the journalist would probably usher Moses and Aaron into the media room for the interview. There would be an agreement that there was only time for six questions because they were on their way to an appointment with Pharaoh.

The journalist's six questions would all focus on one subject. He would not be interested in the many rumors that had circulated about Moses and his family background. He would not address the

---

[118] Exodus 4:31.

Egyptian tabloid stories about Moses' new wife and their relationship. He would not even ask about the allegations of the murder of the Egyptian overseer or the outstanding warrant for Moses' arrest. Instead, all six questions would be about the One called יהוה. Of course, the journalist would dig deep into his training and choose the six most famous interrogatory questions of all time: who, what, when, where, why, and how.

Journalist: Who is יהוה?

Moses: He is the Elohim of our fathers, the Elohim of Abraham, the Elohim of Isaac, and the Elohim of Jacob.[119]

Journalist: What does יהוה want to do for us?

Moses: He has seen the oppression and heard the cry of His people and He has come down to rescue us from the hand of the Egyptians.[120]

Journalist: When does יהוה plan to carry out this rescue?

Moses: He is doing it now![121]

Journalist: Where is יהוה planning to take us?

Moses: יהוה is taking us out of Egypt and into a land flowing with milk and honey; the land of the Canaanites, Hittites, Amorites, Perizzites, Hivites, and Jebusites.[122]

---

[119] Exodus 3:6.
[120] Exodus 3:8.
[121] Exodus 3:10.
[122] Exodus 3:8.

Journalist: Why is יהוה doing this for us?

Moses: Because יהוה made a promise to our ancestors Abraham, Isaac, and Jacob, and because He hears, sees, and acts.[123]

Journalist: How will יהוה do this miraculous thing?

Moses: Through His name![124]

I can imagine that he would want to ask a seventh question to get more thoughts on the *"through His name"* statement, but Aaron would end the interview and insist that the time was up. I imagine that Moses would stand up and say something like this:

I have an appointment with Pharaoh so I have no more time for questions. But let me leave you with something to ponder. When I asked יהוה what was the name I should tell the people and He answered me, there was a promise of action through His name. He revealed Himself through His name as the One who is willing "TO BE!" Think of His name this way: He was, He is, and He will be! He is not limited by time or circumstance. He can never be too late or too early. He cannot be contained, controlled, shut out, locked up, or ignored. Past failures, present threats, and future challenges cannot stop the promise of His name in action. As you see the miracles that are about to take place in your midst here in Egypt, just bow your head and say:

---

[123] Exodus 3:9, 17.
[124] Exodus 3:14.

הָיָה הֹוֶה וְיִהְיֶה *haiyah hoveh*[125] *veyihyeh*
He was, He is and He shall be.
He is יהוה.

After an interview like that I would bow my head, thank
יהוה and start packing for my trip out of bondage!

I hope you still have your shoes off so there can be no
barrier between you and the holy ground we are on right now. I
trust that you understand, to the best of your ability, the meaning of
יהוה as the great "I AM." Now let's continue our study of this
pivotal and powerful verse in Exodus 3:15.

The Application

The third portion of the passage I want to focus on is the
last statement in Exodus 3:15, which is sometimes translated as,
"This is My memorial-name to all generations." Our young Jewish
boy would read about this important phrase in his new Stone
Edition Chumash. I am impressed by the lengths to which Jewish
commentators will go to maintain the ban on the name. I hope they
are equally as impressed by the lengths to which this book will go
to expose and undo this unbiblical ban. Here is the commentary:

> *This is My Name forever.* Since the word לעלם
> [*le'olam*] is spelled without the customary ו it can be
> pronounced לעלם to conceal. This implies that the
> Divine Name should not be pronounced as it is
> spelled. God continued, *"this is My remembrance"*
> meaning that He taught Moses to pronounce the
> Name as *Adonoy.*
>
> Rashi from Midrash Pesachim 50a[126]

---

[125] This rare form appears only in Ecclesiastes 2:22 and Nehemiah 6:6. A variant form *hoyah* is found in Exodus 9:3.
[126] The Stone Edition Chumash, edited by Rabbi Nosson Scherman/Rabbi Meir Zlotowitz. Brooklyn, New York: Mesorah Publications, 2001, page 305, paragraph 15.

Before you get frustrated, understand that Rashi is saying that the Hebrew word לעלם (le'olam), which means *forever,* actually means *concealed.* I cannot pass up the opportunity to interact with the great Jewish commentator Rashi on this verse. Rashi is an acronym for Rabbi Shlomo ben Yitzchak. I must admit this is a daunting task; Rashi is considered to be one of the best Tanach commentators of the Middle Ages. I can understand why English translators conceded to the Jewish commentators, especially with linguistic challenges like this one. It is much easier to just follow the traditional opinion of the majority than to dig for the truth. I am going to take you through my process of discovery on this issue not knowing the outcome. In other words, as I am writing this section I do not know what I will find regarding Rashi's line of reasoning. Here we go!

I will begin by checking my Hebrew Bible to confirm two things. I want to know if the word לעלם (le'olam, forever) in this verse is written without the customary ו (the word is usually spelled לעולם). Do you see the difference? This word is very common and appears with its "full-spelling" more than 400 times in the Tanach. I want to check the *Masorah* of the Masoretic text, which are the notes in the margins of my Hebrew Tanach. The Scribes were very strict about noting variations in spelling. These notes provide another layer of discovery. As I examine Exodus 3:15 I find the following note regarding this word that Rashi is commenting about. I see לעלם with several Hebrew letters in the margin that give me some guidance; they are יח חס י מנה בתור. These Hebrew letters are full of information that explains one aspect of Rashi's argument. (If you are interested in learning how to decipher these scribal annotations, in Appendix C I have listed a book that explains them. It is *The Masorah of Biblia Hebraica Stuttgartensia,* by Paige H. Kelly and Daniel S. Mynatt.)

These letters tell me that this word is written in *"defective spelling"* 18 times. This means that the word is occasionally spelled differently, but carries the same meaning. The note goes on to explain that 10 of the 18 are in the Torah (five books of Moses). Now I want to find these 10 places where our word of interest occurs in the Torah. It only makes sense to find out if Moses uses this "revelatory" spelling in other verses and what it means. Sure enough, I have found all 10 occurrences of this *defective spelling* of לעלם in the Torah.[127] Now let's look at these passages to see if there is any *"special revelation"* or *"concealing"* taking place. I encourage you to check each verse for yourself to see if *"to conceal"* could or should take the place of *"forever."* Here are two from the Torah for you to consider:

> [The Sabbath] is a sign between Me and the sons of Israel forever [לעלם, *le'olam*]. . . .
>
> EXODUS 31:17

If I follow Rashi's interpretation of this word in this form, it means that I should read it as *conceal* instead of *forever*. It would be a tragedy if the Sabbath was to be *concealed* rather than to be a visible sign *forever*. Here is a second verse for us to consider:

> Remember Abraham, Isaac, and Israel, Your servants to whom You swore by Yourself, and said to them, 'I will multiply your descendants as the stars of the heavens, and all this land of which I have spoken I will give to your descendants, and they shall inherit it forever' [לעלם, *le'olam*].
>
> EXODUS 32:13

I know that a lot of people would love to use Rashi's interpretation as an argument that the promise to inherit the land is to be *concealed* rather than last *forever*.

The second thing I will do is check to see if I can find the word in this form, in the exact way it is written in our verse, with the meaning *to conceal*. The word for *conceal* is עלם (*'alam*) and it is used 28 times in various forms throughout the Tanach; nine of

---

[127] See Genesis 3:22, 6:3, Exodus 3:15, 15:18, 21:6, 31:17, 32:13, Leviticus 25:46, Deuteronomy 5:29, 32:40.

those times are in the Torah. Of the 28 times it is used, not once is it preceded by a ל (thereby making it לעלם). So we see that there is not one time that the word spelled לעלם means *to conceal*. [128]

The third thing I want to know is if there is a *Qere-Ketiv* note in the Masorah regarding this word. These are places where the scribes wrote one word, but instructed the reader in the notes to pronounce the word differently than it is written. This phenomenon exists throughout the Tanach. There is a circle written over the word and a special note ק or קר that lets the reader know to read a word one way but to pronounce it a different way. There is no *Qere-Ketiv* note for our special word.

An important comment needs to be made here. There is no such *Qere-Ketiv* note on any of the 6,828 occurrences of the name יהוה in the Masoretic text. In other words, there is no circle written over the name and instruction within the manuscript that says, "Read it this way but pronounce it differently or as Adonai/Adonoy." Some scholars argue that the name is an example of *Qere Perpetuum,* which means they believe that this word is always to be written one way and read differently. Sometimes with a *Qere Perpetuum* there is a scribal note for the word and sometimes there is no note. However, there is not one time in the entire Tanach where there is a note above the name יהוה that indicates a *Qere-Ketiv* or a *Qere Perpetuum*.

Finally, I will look for any evidence of a witness that says Moses was told by יהוה to say *"Adonoy"* instead of יהוה. It is clear that there is no such command here or anywhere else in Scripture.

I am aware that many people argue that Moses was given the prohibition against pronouncing the name via the Oral Law, not through the written text. I choose not to give credence to the Oral Law because there is no way to argue with the rabbis about something that is not in the biblical text. I would like to strongly encourage you to do your own research on the tradition of the Oral

---

[128] One word for *conceal* is העלים (*he'lim*), as in 2 Kings 4:27; with a lamed it would be *le-ha'alim*. The rabbis were interpreting לעלם (*le'olam*) as a shortened form of the hifil in which the hey is dropped, making it *le'alim*. Thanks, Nehemia!

Law and how it has affected biblical interpretation. I believe the written text was meant to be read and spoken aloud to the ancient Israelites every seven years.[129] There was no commentator to interrupt the reader and explain to the people, "What יהוה *really* meant was . . ." The Torah is perfect and complete, without commentary, in its plain meaning.

Look at the following *two* verses and decide if there is any justification for using the Oral Law.

> You shall not add to the word which I am commanding you, nor take away from it, that you may keep the commandments of יהוה your Elohim which I command you.
>
> DEUTERONOMY 4:2

> Whatever I command you, you shall be careful to do; you shall not add to nor take away from it.
>
> DEUTERONOMY 12:32

Now I would like to share some important *biblical* information about this verse that will help you understand the significance of speaking/mentioning the name יהוה. The issue we have to deal with is the phrase at the end of Exodus 3:15, which says: *"This is My name forever, and this is my memorial-name to all generations."*

The question is how can a name be categorized as a *memorial?* We need to delve into a bit of linguistic, grammatical, and technical information in order to understand this pivotal verse.[130] The word translated as *"My memorial-name"* is זכרי (*zikri*), but normally we would expect to find the word זיכרון (*zikron*). For example, this word is first used in Exodus 12:14 in reference to the celebration of Passover: *"Now this day will be a memorial* [זיכרון, *zikron*] *to you."* Of the 24 times it is used in Scripture, seven are in

---

[129] Deuteronomy 31:9-13.
[130] Nehemia Gordon, "The Pronunciation of the Name," www.Karaite-Korner.org.

Exodus. However, the word used in Exodus 3:15 is not זיכרון (*zikron*), but זכרי (*zikri*).

This special word is the key that unlocks the meaning of this unique verse. This is the only time in the entire Hebrew Bible that זכרי (*zikri*) is used in this *exact* form as a noun in the masculine singular construct with a first singular suffix. It appears in different forms the other 23 times. Before we look at the noun form of this word, we can glean some important information by first looking at the word as a verb.

The root is זכר (*zekher*), which means "to remember" and encompasses *two* meanings in one word. It can mean to remember with your *mind* or with your *mouth*. Here is an example where it is used for both *mind* and *mouth* in the same verse:

> Only keep me in mind [זכר, *zekher*] when it goes well with you, and please do me a kindness by mentioning [זכר, *zekher*] me to Pharaoh and get me out of this house.
>
> GENESIS 40:14

When זכר (*zekher*) is used in the *hiphil* (or causative) conjugation, the translators almost always render it as *"mention."* A very clear example is found in Exodus 23:13: *". . . and do not mention the name of other gods, nor let them be heard from your mouth."* As you can see, the translators use *"mention"* for the *hiphil* of זכר (*zekher*). However, they have chosen to use *remembered* for the same word and conjugation in a very interesting verse that is connected to Exodus 3:15. I am certain that many people who read this book will ask, *"Is all of this technical stuff really necessary?"* My response is that it depends on how confident you want to be in His holy word. You see, I think that some people want the fruit without the labor. Because of what you have studied so far, let me share with you what I call a bona fide blessing from heaven based on the word זכר (*zekher*).

If I ask the average religious person if blessings are important, he will answer with a resounding *"Yes! The blessings from our Heavenly Father are important."* Everybody seems to be looking for blessings, so there is preaching, promising, praying, begging, and even manipulating for blessings. The same people who ask, *"Does this name and all of this study really matter?"* will surely say that blessings matter. In His wisdom, יהוה stated a guaranteed way for blessings to come. Put on your translator's hat and read the following verse knowing that the word *mentioned* is from the first person singular *hiphil* form of זכר (*zekher*):

> In every place where I cause My name to be mentioned [אזכיר, *azkir*], I will come to you and bless you.
>
> EXODUS 20:24

In this verse most English translators disregard the grammatical information in order to conceal the mention of the name! They usually translate it this way: *". . . in every place where I cause my name to be remembered, there I will come and bless you."* Open your English Bible and see how this verse is translated. The same word and verb conjugation are translated differently when it comes to the mention of the name יהוה. There are 41 other examples of the use of this same word and conjugation.[131] You might enjoy seeing some examples of what the translators do in these cases.

Actually there are many verses that can shed further light on the biblical meaning of this word in this context.[132] Notice the following verse in Hosea, in light of what you have just learned, and make your own *"translator's decision,"* based on the Hebrew text.

> Even יהוה, the Elohim of Hosts, יהוה is His זכרו [*zikro*].
>
> HOSEA 12:5

---

[131] For example, Joshua 23:7, 1 Samuel 4:18, Isaiah 12:4, Isaiah 19:17, Isaiah 26:13.

[132] See also Hosea 12:5 and Job 18:17. Both verses use the exact same word זכר (*zikro*).

If there is an agenda of not wanting the people to "connect the dots" regarding mentioning the name, how would you translate this verse? Clearly, such an agenda must exist with the following three English translations:

> Even the LORD, the God of hosts, the LORD is His name.
>
> New American Standard Bible (NASB)

> Yet the LORD, the God of Hosts, must be invoked as "LORD."
>
> Jewish Publication Society (JPS, verse 6)

> Even the LORD God of hosts; the LORD is his memorial.
>
> King James Version (KJV)

Can you see the bias in the translations of this verse? The NASB completely changes the word to make it look as though the verse uses the Hebrew word for *name* when in fact, as we have already shown, it is זכרו (*zikro*). The JPS really helps by reminding you to substitute the title LORD for the name. Where is there room for that interpretation in the Hebrew word זכרו (*zikro*)? The KJV is closest to the original, but still veils the word in the unclear term *memorial*. As you can see, checking several different English versions of a verse can help us understand the thinking and practice of translators. Here is my version, which will always be less elegant linguistically, but will be more accurate according to Hebrew grammar.

> And יהוה, the Elohim of Hosts, יהוה is His mention.
>
> HOSEA 12:6 in Hebrew (Keith Johnson Version)

Now let's go back to Exodus 3:15. You might be surprised to see how the English translators seem to pick and choose when they want to *remember* and *mention* the meaning of our word.

In Exodus 3:15 the words *"My memorial-name"* (זכרי, *zikri*) should have been translated as *"My mention."* If I had been on the committee that translated the Hebrew Tanach into English, I would have literally stood on the table and insisted that this verse be translated as follows:

> And יהוה furthermore said to Moses, Thus you shall say to the sons of Israel, יהוה, the Elohim of your fathers, the Elohim of Abraham, the Elohim of Isaac, and the Elohim of Jacob, has sent me to you. This is My name forever and this is My mention [how my name is to be *spoken*] to all generations.
>
> EXODUS 3:15 (Keith Johnson Version)

I believe people could and would then see that the ban against pronouncing or mentioning His name is in direct conflict with this eternal command. In other words, we are required to mention His name יהוה forever and, as we are told elsewhere, we are forbidden to mention the names of other gods! In order to receive the blessing associated with the name יהוה we have to obey an everlasting commandment—we must mention His name!

After all that hard work let's have a little "fun" with this word זכרי (*zikri*). There are actually several men in the Bible who have this name. One in particular caught my attention. Second Chronicles 17:16 *mentions* a man named זכרי (*zikri*) and he had a son who "volunteered" for יהוה. Can you imagine זכרי (*zikri*) constantly *mentioning* the name יהוה and explaining its importance to his son from the time he was a young child? Most likely, when it came time for the son to volunteer for יהוה, he did not hesitate because he knew the One whom his father זכרי (*zikri*) had been *mentioning* for as long as he could remember.

> . . . and next to him Amasiah the son of Zichri, who volunteered for יהוה, and with him 200,000 valiant warriors.
>
> 2 CHRONICLES 17:16

This word זכרי (*zikri*) should be teaching us to *mention* יהוה with no shame. Hopefully we can find a whole army of people who will volunteer to do the same!

I hope the exegesis of this passage in which יהוה reveals His name to Moses has helped you understand why we must *remember* to *mention* His name! The unique personal name יהוה has been preserved in the Hebrew Scriptures. He has told us that this is His name forever. In fact, יהוה requires His name to be *"mentioned,"* not only by us, but by every generation to come. When He shared His name with Moses He had us in mind too. Don't you think we should get busy remembering and mentioning Him?

> Your שם [*shem,* name], O יהוה, is לעולם [*le'olam,* everlasting], your זכרך [*zikreka,* your mention], O יהוה, throughout all generations.
>
> PSALMS 135:13 (Keith Johnson Version)

I chose the above verse for two reasons. First, because it uses both Hebrew words that we studied in Exodus 3:15, along with two others that you have already learned. Second, it is the verse that our graphic designer chose for the cover of this book. Did you notice how many times יהוה is included in Psalms 135? Great job Reneé!

I also wanted to help you gauge how far you have come in reading a little Hebrew! In this verse, the words *your mention* (זכרך, *zikreka*) are a correct translation,[133] just like *my mention* (זכרי, *zikri*) but with a different suffix. I hope you are encouraged by your newly acquired left-handed language skills.

Back to the Blessing!

Now that we have labored to understand the significance of *mentioning* versus *remembering,* let's enjoy the blessing that can

---

[133] See Psalms 6:5 in the NASB version, which also uses *mention* rather than *remembrance* based on the Hebrew word *zeker*.

come from the fruit of our lips when we mention the remarkable name יהוה. There is a verse in Second Samuel that calls for our attention regarding the blessing that comes with mentioning His name:

> Now it was told King David, saying, "יהוה has blessed the house of Obed-edom and all that belongs to him, on account of the ark of Elohim."
>
> 2 SAMUEL 6:12

When we read the context surrounding this verse, we find that the ark of Elohim was temporarily "stored" at Obed-edom's house while David decided what to do with this holy object. During the three months of this temporary storage a blessing fell upon Obed-edom and his entire household. If we do just a little more digging, we can find an explanation for this blessing:

> And David arose and went with all the people who were with him to Baale-Judah, to bring up the ark of Elohim which is called by the Name, the very name יהוה of hosts who is enthroned above the cherubim.
>
> 2 SAMUEL 6:2

I imagine that as soon as the ark which was "called by the Name" arrived at the house of Obed-edom everything began to change. I am sure that family, friends, and neighbors wanted to get a glimpse of this amazing object. I can also imagine that when people asked what this glorious ark was called, Obed-Edom simply called it "by the Name." There is no secret about why the blessing coincided with the arrival of the ark of Elohim. The ark was called by the name יהוה.

There is a biblical explanation for the blessing that was given to the house of Obed-edom. Can you guess what verse I will use to explain the blessing?

In every place where I cause My name to be mentioned [אזכיר *azkir*], I will come to you and bless you.

EXODUS 20:24 (Keith Johnson Version)

When the Name stopped at the house of Obed-edom, the blessing automatically arrived with it. Are you open to having that name stop at your house? If you are, then make room for the blessing that will accompany it.

I hope that by now you are a little more comfortable when you see this name יהוה written from right to left in the Hebrew manuscripts. Now you are ready to learn how to mention or pronounce this awesome, blessing-giving name. If you jumped ahead and missed building the necessary foundation, then you have short-changed yourself. But if you have waded through this process of interaction with the biblical text and with the important historical foundational information, you can look forward to receiving what I call a bona fide blessing from mentioning "The Name."

הַלְלוּ אֶת שֵׁם יְהוָה

Praise the name of the LORD.

ח

CHET

CHAPTER EIGHT

THE AWESOME ANSWER

Check out the first verse of Psalms 135 above. It is part of the first line of Hebrew text shown on the cover of this book. The Hebrew clearly says to praise the name יְהוָה, but the English says to praise the name *of the* LORD. How can we praise His name if all we have is a substitute title? How can we praise His name if we are forbidden to pronounce it? How can we mention His name if we don't know how to say it? How did Jeremiah expect people to vow in the name if they didn't know how to proclaim it?[134] How could Jesus expect the multitude on that famous mountainside to *hallow* the name of our Father in heaven if they didn't know what it was? By now you may be asking these same questions. This chapter will give you the awesome answer so you can pronounce and proclaim the name that we are called to praise!

I was almost deterred from writing this book when I became aware of the many theories about *the deep and hidden secrets to pronouncing the Divine Name*. I would like to take this opportunity to say that I am willing to look at any evidence that challenges the information in this book. There are legitimate debates on how

---

[134] Jeremiah 12:16

letters and vowels were pronounced in ancient Israel and, to be honest, we are at a disadvantage. No ancient audio recordings exist that allow us to hear the exact pronunciation of what has been historically called the Shem Hameforash (the explicit name).[135]

This book contains the most up-to-date information currently available on the subject of the Divine Name. I appreciate the many people who have made this topic of the name יְהֹוָה a priority. I always try to balance my own passion with a humble heart and mind. Now that I have given you my disclaimer, let's get back to work.

Today we have important biblical and historical evidence which reveals that, before the imposition of the famous ban, the pronunciation and use of the name were required in worship and used in everyday life. Following are *two* examples from the Bible and *two* historic examples from the Jewish Talmud.[136]

> Speak to Aaron and his sons, saying, 'Thus you shall bless the sons of Israel. You shall say to them:
>
> יְהֹוָה bless you, and keep you;
>
> יְהֹוָה make his face shine on you, and be gracious to you;
>
> יְהֹוָה lift up his countenance on you, and give you peace.'
>
> NUMBERS 6:24–26

The significance of pronouncing His name in these verses has already been discussed. The following passage indicates how the ancient Israelites used the name as a blessing in daily life.

---

[135] Synonymous with *Shem Hameyuhad*, 'the Unique Name,' and generally held to be identical with the Tetragrammaton, uttered as written, v. Sanh. (Sonc. ed.) page 408, n. 1.

[136] The Talmud (Hebrew תַּלְמוּד talmūd, "instruction, learning," from the root *lmd*, meaning "teach, study") is a record of rabbinic discussions pertaining to Jewish law, ethics, customs, and history. It is a central text of mainstream Judaism.

Now behold, Boaz came from Bethlehem and said to the reapers, "May יְהֹוָה be with you." And they answered him, "May יְהֹוָה bless you."

RUTH 2:4

The following are two extra-biblical references:

In the Temple the name was pronounced.

TALMUD SOTAH 37b

It was ordained that a man should greet his friends by mentioning the name.

TALMUD BERACHOTH 54a

As you can see from all four examples, people were *expected* to pronounce the name יְהֹוָה. Many other references in biblical and historical documents reveal that the name יְהֹוָה was commonly spoken by the people throughout biblical times and until the famous ban was imposed.

I hope that by now you are familiar enough with seeing יְהֹוָה that you noticed there are some very small, but important, dots and symbols placed above and below the name. These are the keys to pronunciation. I refer to these dots and symbols, which are called vowel points, as "the preachers of the name."

You are about to enter the congregation of those who listen and learn from these powerful preachers that proclaim the pronunciation of our Heavenly Father's name. Unfortunately, you must first walk past the protestors who will urge you to dismiss the message of these persuasive preachers. I will try to balance my excitement about introducing you to these preachers of the name, with the need to address the protestors' objections.

Here is just one of the many messages you might hear from the protestors:

THE NAME OF THE LORD: In all other editions the name of the LORD JHVH is printed with nikkud (vowels) which may mislead the reader to read this name as it is strictly forbidden to do. This name of the LORD has to be read in the form of "Adonoot." In the Koren edition the name is printed without vowels: this eliminates the possibility of the forbidden reading and emphasizes the holiness of this name.[137]

This comment is from the publishers of a Hebrew-English Bible printed in Jerusalem! Should we listen to the protesters and return to reading, pronouncing, and praying *titles* rather than the actual *name* that was placed in Jerusalem forever? Absolutely not! Let's continue our journey!

Each chapter you have read to this point has been an important building block, like the huge stones under the Western Wall of the Temple in Jerusalem. With these blocks in place, we can now begin to build above ground. What you are about to read will shake the very foundations of tradition and translation, and may inspire you to make a life-changing decision. If you have skipped ahead to this chapter, then you are building without a solid foundation. We know what happens to a house that is built without the proper foundation.

As we continue building we will add vital information to our solid foundation. It is unfortunate that many people of faith don't seem to be concerned about adding knowledge to their faith. I have been encouraged by the work of many scholars who have dedicated their lives to gaining a better understanding of Scripture. It is very beneficial to interact with those who have spent so much time and energy learning about this subject.

With this in mind, I am certainly aware that the information in this chapter will be challenged by some of the "scholars" of the churches and the synagogues. I must say, however, that I did not write this book primarily for them. This chapter is for those of you

---

[137] The Jerusalem Bible, Korén Publishers Jerusalem Ltd., Jerusalem, 2000.

who want to understand the handwriting of the *two* scribes who reveal the name!

The audiences I hope to reach are the people who want to receive the inheritance of this name. I realize, of course, that I will have to deal with the opinions of the scholars and protestors in order to explain the pronunciation of the name. In the final analysis, it will not be me, but the Hebrew manuscripts themselves that will answer the crucial question of how to pronounce the name. I will make every effort to explain this topic as simply and clearly as I can. Make no mistake, the simplicity of the explanation is backed up by the most up-to-date information available. Unfortunately, this information has been buried under layers of language, culture, and religious bias, and kept under wraps by the enforcers of *tradition* and *translation*. The time has come to uncover this information so all people can have access to the name יְהֹוָה *again!*

Before I answer the question of how to pronounce the name directly from the Hebrew text, I first want to give some basic but important information that explains how the pronunciation was preserved. According to most biblical scholars, Hebrew words were written without vowels until the time of the Masoretes[138] (approximately 700-900 C.E.). These scribes made it their life mission to supply the proper "vowel pointing" (voice) to every word in the Hebrew Bible. It is crucial to understand that the Masoretes did not *create* the pronunciation of Hebrew words; they merely devised a vowel system that represented the correct pronunciation. Their job was to add vowels to the consonants so the words of the Hebrew scrolls could be pronounced correctly by anyone who read them.

When I traveled to Israel in 2002 I was able to obtain an ancient Torah scroll for my personal study. It is quite a challenge to open the scroll and read the words without vowel signs. However,

---

[138] The Masoretes (בעלי המסורה ba'alei hamasorah) were groups of scribes and textual scholars working between the 7th and 11th centuries, based primarily in the cities of Tiberias and Jerusalem, as well as in Babylonia (present-day Iraq).

for literally thousands of years that is what people have done. In fact, in Israel most Hebrew words on billboards, places of business, and even newspapers do not have vowel signs, yet people are able to read the words without difficulty. For example, can you read this popular verse from the Torah?

> Y shll lv th Lrd yr lhm wth ll yr hrt nd wth ll yr sl nd wth ll yr mght.

If I were a Masorete it would be my job to add the vowels to the consonants so even if you didn't know this verse you could read it correctly. By adding the English vowel system to these words this verse would read,

> You shall love the LORD your Elohim with all your heart and with all your soul and with all your might.
>
> DEUTERONOMY 6:5

We should be forever grateful to the scribes for their labor of love. They developed a vowel system that made it possible to correctly pronounce every word in the Hebrew Bible. They knew every letter, word, phrase, paragraph, and book inside and out! Once you learn the vowel symbols, the words come alive! You can easily learn some of these important symbols and be able to proclaim this heavenly name just the way the scribes wrote it!

Before continuing, I must bring up two additional points. First, there is evidence from a number of different sources that suggests that the vowels were added to Hebrew texts much earlier than many scholars have claimed. This subject would need to be covered in a separate study. For the purposes of this book I have decided to share with you the information I have seen personally. Second, there are some who argue that no vowels should be added to the name; in other words, the name יהוה should be spoken without vowels. There are two words that best describe my response to the approach of pronouncing the name without vowels: good luck.

The Two Textual Witnesses

For our purposes, the key point is how the Masoretic scribes dealt with the vowel points for the four Hebrew letters יהוה. They had a deep reverence for the name יהוה, yet they also were under the rabbinical ban not to speak it or write it in its fully-vocalized form. This does not mean that they did not *know* the pronunciation or the *"full spelling."* In fact, in *two* of the oldest vocalized Hebrew manuscripts the Masoretes actually added the complete vowel points into the name of our Heavenly Father. Consequently, His name can be spoken by you and me today!

First we will peer into the oldest complete vocalized Hebrew manuscript in the world: the Leningrad Codex B19A.[139] A modern printing that accurately reproduces the Leningrad manuscript is the *Biblia Hebraica Stuttgartensia* (BHS).[140] The BHS is a scientific edition of this manuscript. I own a BHS that I took to Jerusalem in 2002. I bought it in seminary and had no idea that the most important name in the universe was right there all the time. It was an amazing and inspiring experience for me when I first saw the complete vowel pointing of the name in my own Hebrew Bible. Do you remember what it looks like from our earlier discussion? If not, take a look again at the handwriting of Shemu'el ben Ya'acob at the end of Chapter One.

Today the printings are not needed since the actual manuscripts themselves are available as lithographic editions. I have been blessed to be able to purchase and study one of these photographed manuscripts. Until 1990 this priceless manuscript was stored behind the Iron Curtain in St. Petersburg, Russia, with scholars having only limited access to it. It was a humbling and exhilarating experience to see the name fully vocalized just as it was written by the scribe in his actual handwriting!

---

[139] The Leningrad Codex is an ancient Hebrew manuscript of the entire Old Testament that is housed in Russia. It was not made available to be photographed until the summer of 1990.
[140] *Biblia Hebraica Stuttgartensia* (edited by K. Elliger and W. Rudolph, et al, Deutsche Bibelgesellschaft Stuttgart 1967/77, 1983). To date, the BHS is the most precise printing of the Hebrew Scriptures, only rarely deviating from the Leningrad Codex.

Everyone who has relied on scholarly opinions regarding this topic should now question how many scholars have ever seen or studied this manuscript. This is the reason I want to encourage a dialogue with the scholars. Just as information from the Dead Sea Scrolls has led to certain "changes of opinion," the text of the Leningrad Codex deserves the same consideration for a new dialogue about the name יהוה.

Now I will address the long-standing "opinion" of the majority of scholars. If you look in most commentaries, Bible dictionaries, or the introductions of most Bibles, you will find a uniform answer to the question of the pronunciation of the name. My ordination Bible states the following:

> To the four consonants YHWH of the Name, which had come to be regarded as too sacred to be pronounced, they attached vowel signs indicating that in its place should be read the Hebrew word *Adonai* meaning "Lord" (or *Elohim* meaning "God").[141]

I can't begin to count how many times I have read essentially this same explanation in books, articles, and Bibles. A story is also told (whether true or not I don't know) that a sixteenth-century German Christian scribe translated the Bible into Latin for the Pope. He is said to have copied the name as it appeared in his Hebrew source document: with the consonants of YHVH and the vowels of Adonai. By doing that he basically coined a hybrid word that has lasted ever since. The problem with this story—and it is huge—is that *in the oldest complete vocalized Hebrew manuscript there are no examples of the consonants of* יהוה *being written with the vowels of* Adonai.

The argument that the vowels of *Adonai* were placed within the consonants יהוה is false and misleading. Remember, the symbols below and above the Hebrew letters represent vowel sounds. Look at the following example for yourself.

---

[141] Metzger, page xii.

The vowels of אֲדֹנָי (*Adonai*) are *hatef patch* אֲ (*ah*), *holem* דֹ (*do*), and *qamets* נָי (*nai*):

$$\text{אֲדֹנָי}$$

The vowels placed with the consonants of יהוה that are used 99 percent of the time in the Leningrad manuscript are *sheva* יְ (*Ye*) and *qamets* וָ (*vah*):

$$\text{יְהֹוָה}$$

If the vowels of Adonai were placed within יהוה, then we would expect to see יֲהוָֹה with a *hatef patch* יֲ under the *yod,* not a *sheva* יְ as it is actually written in the Leningrad Codex.

There is only one place in the entire Leningrad manuscript where we can find a witness that comes close to supporting this argument. In Psalms 144:15 יהוה appears with a שׁ (shin), which is a relative particle, before the name (שֶׁיֲהוָֹה). This is the only time a *hatef patch* vowel is used with a *yod* יֲ in the name! But even this one example does not have all the vowels of אֲדֹנָי (*Adonai*). The most important thing this one witness proves is that if the Masoretes wanted to place the vowels of *Adonai* into the name, as the majority of scholars claim, they certainly could have done it. Rather, we see well over 6,000 times that they use the *sheva* יְ under the first letter of the name.

The scribe of the Leningrad Codex consistently left out the middle vowel of the name 6,778 times. Since the rabbis "commanded" that the name must not be pronounced, 99 percent of the time it was written with incomplete vowel points so it *could not* be pronounced properly. The *one* time the scribe wrote a *hatef patch* instead of a *sheva* in the name clearly does not validate the theory that the vowels of *Adonai* were ever written with the consonants יהוה. The scholars are correct in saying that the Jews *say* "Adonai" when they come to the name in the text, but they are wrong to say or imply that it was *written* that way or that the vowels of Adonai are in any sense a guide for the correct pronunciation of יהוה.

One reason for the confusion is that some Hebrew Bible publishers have freely *modified* the name in a number of ways. Some modern printings always leave the vowels out of the name (earlier we read one example of this in the Korén edition of the Tanach). There are also some who actually use the vowels of *Adonai* in the name. But none of these publications is based on the earliest vocalized Hebrew manuscripts. They are Hebrew equivalents to our versions that freely *changed* the name. I encourage you to find a *Biblia Hebraica Stuttgartensia,* or even visit a seminary library to look at a lithograph of the Leningrad Codex B19A.[142] It is this manuscript that witnesses unequivocally to the true pronunciation of the name!

The Guessing Game

I can say with confidence that verifying the hotly-debated opinions about the pronunciation of the name יהוה is worth the time and energy it takes to get it right. At the very least we should insist that any argument must be based on *solid textual evidence.* Considering what you have learned to this point, would you agree that the name יהוה deserves more than just a guess? Unfortunately, when it comes to the most popular opinion about the pronunciation of this magnificent name, a guess is the best most scholars have given us. Here are *two* opinions of many that you can read:

> While it is almost if not quite certain that the Name was originally pronounced "Yahweh," this pronunciation was not indicated when the Masoretes added vowel sounds to the consonantal Hebrew text.[143]

---

[142] The Leningrad Codex, also known as LB19A, is now available as *The Leningrad Codex: A Facsimile Edition.* D. N. Freedman (editor), Wm. B. Eerdmans Publishing Co. 1998.
[143] Metzger, page xii.

I personally appreciate the honesty of the *Anchor Bible Dictionary*, which explains:

> The pronunciation of *yhwh* as Yahweh is a scholarly guess.[144]

Do you believe that the Father wants his people to simply *guess* how to say His name? The majority of scholars have played the guessing game and passed down their conjectures to us. Those who say His name is *Yahweh* base their argument on information from sources outside the actual Hebrew text. Their primary source is Theodoret of Cyrus, a Church Father who lived in the fifth century C.E. He wrote the following concerning the name יהוה:

> The Samaritans call Him IABE. . . .[145]

The ancient Samaritans called the Creator יָפֶה (*Yafeh*), meaning "the beautiful one." In Samaritan Hebrew the letter *pe* (פ) is often replaced by *bet* (ב). One theory is that the Samaritans told Theodoret that יהוה is called *Yafeh*, "the beautiful one," but because of their particular accent it came out as *Yabe*.[146]

Most scholars claim that the *b* in *Iabe* (pronounced Yahbay) is a distortion of a Hebrew *vav* (ו) and that the first *hey* (ה) of יהוה was dropped because Greek does not have an *h* sound in the middle of a word. As a result most scholars convert the Samaritan *Iabe* back into Hebrew as *Yahweh*.[147] However, in 6,828 occurrences, not one time is the name written as *Yahbey, Yahvay* or *Yahwey* in the Hebrew manuscript. This is a plain, biblical fact—not a scholarly guess!

---

[144] D. N. Freedman, ed., *The Anchor Bible Dictionary,* Vol. 6, page 1011.

[145] Theodoret of Cyrus, *Quaestio 15 in Exodus: A commentary on the pronunciation of the name by the Samaritans* (in Latin).

[146] Thanks to Meir Rekhavi for providing this information about the Samaritans to Nehemia who shared it with me.

[147] Nehemia Gordon, "The Pronunciation of the Name," www.Karaite-Korner.org.

One great blessing of studying biblical Hebrew is that I have been given access to some of the same information as the scholars. Checking the facts is very informative. If you are willing to take a short walk through the garden of Hebrew grammar you will learn why the "scholarly guess" regarding the popular pronunciation *"Yahweh"* is flawed. I remember how excited I was when Nehemia explained the grammatical principles that demonstrate why יהוה cannot be pronounced *"Yahweh."* Here is a small portion of what he shared with me:

> This means that the scholarly assumption that YHVH is the *piel* or *hifil* form of HYH *to be* is impossible since this verb does not exist in those conjugations. In other words, according to biblical Hebrew Yahweh is a non-existent verbal form. So why do modern scholars universally identify the name YHVH as some fictitious verb that defies the rules of Hebrew grammar? There is a twofold reason for this. First, the non-existent *piel* or *hifil* form would result in YHVH meaning "he that causes to be." This fits perfectly with the theological preconceptions of modern scholars. Second, the *piel* or *hifil* form Yahweh fits with the testimony of Theodoret concerning the Samaritan pronunciation of the name.[148]

Nehemia has done a significant amount of research on this topic and I hope he will one day make it available in a scholarly publication. In the meantime, this is my best effort for those who want the information now in layman's terms.

The Hebrew verb system consists of seven different forms or *conjugations*. These forms give different shades of meaning to words. The root can be the same but the *conjugation* is different based on the desired meaning of the word and the verbal pattern.

---

[148] Nehemia Gordon, "The Pronunciation of the Name," www.Karaite-Korner.org.

Some verbs can be conjugated in all seven forms and some only use two or three forms. Many scholars suggest that the meaning of the verb that is the basis of the name יהוה should be rendered as "He that causes to be." To back up their claim they insert the vowels of the *piel* or *hifil* conjugations, which would create a word pronounced *"Yahweh."* In other words, biblical scholars placed vowels into the Tetragrammaton *making up* a verbal form to match their *theory,* or more accurately, their *"guess."* The problem is that in the entire Hebrew Bible this verb only occurs with two conjugations: *qal* and *niphal.*

Another pronunciation problem with *Yahweh* (apart from a unique form that will be explained later) is that no people in the Hebrew Bible have names with יה (*yod hey*), pronounced *"Yah,"* as a prefix. The closest is *Yahedai* in 1 Chronicles 2:47, but the difference in this name is that the second syllable has a vowel (הֶ), which is pronounced *heh,* rather than having a silent *sheva* that would create the *"Yah"* pronunciation as in the hypothetical name *Yahweh.* There are, on the other hand, *many* names with *yah* or *yahu* as a suffix, such as Yesha-YaHu (Isaiah), Eli-YaHu (Elijah), Yermi-YaHu (Jeremiah), Tsidqi-YaHu (Zedekiah), Athal-YaHu (Athaliah), Hizqi-YaHu (Hezekiah), and Yoshi-YaHu (Josiah). Between the first and second Temple periods the ending of these names was shortened to *yah.* Let's add a little more depth to the issue of the Divine Name incorporated into the beginning and ending of Hebrew names:

Many Hebrew names incorporate part of the divine name as part of a compound name. For example, Yᵉhoshua (Joshua) means "YHVH saves," while Yeshayahu (Isaiah) also means "YHVH saves." We can see that the divine name, when incorporated into other names, is Yeho- when it appears at the beginning of a name and -yahu at the end of the name. Proponents of the name as Yahweh often cite the ending form -yahu as proof of their pronunciation. There are two problems with this.

First, the divine element -yahu is not consistent with the pronunciation Yahweh. Instead it might suggest some such pronunciation as Yahuvah but not Yahweh. In Hebrew there is even less similarity between *Yahweh* יהוה and יָהוּ -*yahu* than there is in English. *Yahweh* יהוה is spelled with a Hebrew vowel called *chataf patach* while -*yahu* יָהוּ has the vowel *kamats*. These are two different vowels with different pronunciations. The difference between these two vowels is like the difference between the "a" in *father* (*chataf patach*) and the "a" in *brawl* (so roughly *kamats* in ancient Hebrew). This is only a mistake that an English or German speaker could make! Secondly, in the name YHVH, the letters YHW- are actually at the beginning of the name, not the end. So if we look to names such as Joshua or Isaiah as our model of reconstructing the pronunciation of the divine name we must choose the pattern Yeho- which is at the beginning of these compound names, not the end.[149]

Another interesting theory is based on a witness by the Jewish historian Josephus, who wrote in Greek and gave this description of the clothing of the High Priest on the Day of Atonement.[150]

A mitre (cap) also of fine linen encompassed his head, which was tied by a blue ribbon, about which there was another golden crown, in which was engraven the sacred name [of God]: it consists of four vowels. However, the high priest did not wear these garments at other times, but a more plain habit; he only did it when he went into the most sacred part

---

[149] Nehemia Gordon, "The Pronunciation of the Name," www.Karaite-Korner.org.
[150] Exodus 39:28-30.

of the temple, which he did but once in a year, on that day when our custom is for all of us to keep a fast to God [Yom Kippur/Day of Atonement].

Wars of the Jews, Book 5, Chapter 5

Those who base their argument on this important witness seem to misunderstand that this was originally written in Greek, or they do not know the basics of the Greek and Hebrew alphabets. There are no Greek letters that correspond to the four Hebrew letters יהוה (*yod, hey, vav, hey*).

The vowels of ancient Greek were much different than the Hebrew vowel system. Biblical Hebrew had nine vowels which do not have exact equivalents in Greek. For example, Hebrew's *vocal sheva* (pronounced like the *i* in "bit") has no equivalent in ancient Greek. So the third letter of the divine name must also be dropped or distorted by the Greek.[151]

Apparently Josephus is trying to help Greek readers understand that the four Hebrew letters of the name are "phonetically" similar to Greek vowels. For those who read Greek, here is a portion of what Josephus wrote: φωνήεντα τέσσαρα (*phonenta tessara*), which means "four vowels."

What makes this even more intriguing is that the Hebrew letters in the name have historically been used as both consonants and vowels. In Hebrew and some other Semitic languages, the term *matres lectionis*[152] refers to the use of certain consonants to indicate a vowel. The letters that function this way in Hebrew are א (*aleph*), ה (*hey*), ו (*vav*) and י (*yod*). Three of these letters (or vowels) make up the name יהוה.

---

[151] Nehemia Gordon, "The Pronunciation of the Name," www.Karaite-Korner.org.
[152] Latin expression meaning "mothers of reading;" singular form: *mater lectionis*. In Hebrew: אֵם קְרִיאָה *mother of reading*.

Josephus is saying that in both Greek and Hebrew the four letters on the mitre of the High Priest can be called vowels even though they are also consonants in Hebrew. This information has led some to argue that in Hebrew the name is pronounced as four vowels and thus they come up with a pronunciation that forces the Greek testimony of Josephus into the Hebrew pronunciation of the Name. You can be sure that the High Priest did not have Greek vowels on the mitre, but Hebrew letters which Josephus is trying to describe to a Greek-speaking and Greek-reading audience.[153]

The bottom line is that there is no Hebrew manuscript witness to the popular name *Yahweh* or *Yahveh!* I have decided to focus on the *direct manuscript evidence* rather than attempt to put the puzzle together with pieces from external sources. As you continue reading, you will understand how significant the two Hebrew manuscripts are as witnesses to the pronunciation of this profound and powerful name.

You can find a plethora of pronunciation possibilities that may *sound good,* but likewise have no Hebrew manuscript evidence or grammatical validity. In my humble opinion, if the explanation of the pronunciation of this magnificent name is not witnessed in the Hebrew manuscripts, then I categorize it as a part of the Hebrew name guessing game. You now have in your hands some foundational linguistic information to ponder regarding the pronunciation possibilities of the fantastic four-letter name יהוה.

No More Guessing

Enough guessing! How is the sanctified name יהוה with its vowels written in the ancient manuscript? The answer is amazing and it's filled with what seems to be intervention and revelation from our Heavenly Father.

When you first see the name יְהֹוָה (*Yehvah*) you might notice that the expected vowel that should follow the first ה (*hey*) is

---

[153] See Josephus' *Antiquities* 11:331 for a second statement about the mitre with the name engraved upon it.

missing. A fundamental rule of Hebrew is that a consonant in the middle of a word is almost always followed by either a vowel or a silent *sheva* (הְ). Sometimes there are silent letters in the middle of a word that have no vowel or *sheva*. One example is the א (*aleph*) in *ber'eshit* בְּרֵאשִׁית (Genesis 1:1). But this is usually not the case with ה (*hey*) in the middle of a word. In biblical Hebrew it is common for ה (*hey*) to be silent at the end of a word, but it is extremely rare to find a silent ה (*hey*) in the middle of a word.[154]

This means that by the grammatical rules of biblical Hebrew the first ה (*hey*) in יהוה must have a vowel. The Masoretes wrote the name without that vowel—יְהוָה (*Yehvah*)—so it could not be pronounced. They were following the "tradition" of not allowing people to speak the name. The question is, what is the missing vowel? Praise יהוה, we have the answer!

The Leningrad Codex gives us *two* major clues to the missing vowel of the name. When the name יהוה and *Adonai* are juxtaposed (next to each other) the Masoretes added the last vowel point of the word אֱלֹהִים (*Elohim*) so that the reader would not say *Adonai* twice. Following are two examples from the English Bible:

> The Lord GOD has given me the tongue of disciples, that I may know how to sustain the weary one with a word.
>
> ISAIAH 50:4

---

[154] Here are *three* biblical names derived from verbs in which the third letter of the root is a *hey*, specifically Asahel עֲשָׂהאֵל (2 Samuel 2:18) Pedahzur פְּדָהצוּר (Numbers 1:10) and Hazael חֲזָהאֵל (2 Kings 8:8). Each of these names is derived from a root whose third letter is a silent *hey* in the past tense masculine form of the verb. Even though this *hey* is silent, it is always written in this form of the verb. The names derived from these verbs preserve that silent *hey* to indicate the linguistic origin of the name to the reader. The name YHVH is derived from the root HYH and in fact the past tense masculine form of this verb does have a silent *hey* as "hayah." If the principle that created a silent *hey* in the above three names were applied to YHVH, we would end up with the final *hey* in YHVH being silent, which is in fact the case. However, this principle would never make the first *hey* silent in the name YHVH because it is not silent in any form of the verb HYH. Thanks Nehemia!

I am sending you to them who are stubborn and obstinate children, and you shall say to them, "Thus says the Lord GOD."

EZEKIEL 2:4

Both of these verses use exactly the same vowel points for *Lord GOD:*

אֲדֹנָי יְהֹוִה
Yehovih Adonai

By now you probably realize that translating the name יהוה as the word *GOD* is man's attempt to keep the name from being spoken. This Masoretic device of adding the vowels of *Elohim* into the name יהוה leads us to the "missing vowel" of the name.

Remember to read from right to left. Notice the word *Yehovih* in the example above; the first vowel is a *sheva* under the *yod* (יְ). This beginning vowel is used in the Divine Name more than 6,000 times in the biblical text. There is no question that the name written in this manuscript starts with the consonant and vowel יְ (pronounced Y^e). The second vowel is a *holem* הֹ over the *hey*. This is pronounced *ho*. This vowel is our biggest clue. The third vowel is a *hireq* וִ under the *vav*. This is pronounced *vih*. If this were the correct pronunciation, it would be "Yehovih." However, this is clearly not the true pronunciation of the name (even so, there is a far better argument for this pronunciation than for Yahweh). The Masoretes only used the last vowel of אֱלֹהִים (*Elohim*) when the name יהוה is next to *Adonai*. This is an example of a unique scribal practice of changing one vowel of a word for the purpose of reminding the reader to say *Elohim* even though he sees יהוה.

There is one more unique example in my Hebrew Bible that I must explain. This is the only example in the entire Leningrad Codex where the Masoretes took the exact vowels from אֱלֹהִים (*Elohim*) and inserted them into the name יהוה. Even the English translations follow a similar practice when the name is directly next to the word *Adonai:*

144

Then Samson called to יהוה and said "Lord GOD. . . ."

JUDGES 16:28

אֲדֹנָי יֱהֹוִה

Here they correctly translated אֲדֹנָי (*Adonai*) as *Lord,* but where the vowels from *Elohim* are inserted into the name יהוה they translated it as *GOD.* English Bibles will almost always render יהוה as *GOD* when it is next to *Adonai* (Lord), even though the word is not *Elohim* and doesn't mean God. This was the Masoretes' way of indicating what the reader should say when he sees these *two* words next to one another.

There are more than 200 examples in the Hebrew text where they changed the vowels within the name because of the ban. Nevertheless, the Masoretes have given us very big clues about the correct spelling and pronunciation of the name. The proof is the full vowel pointing of the name יהוה, which we find numerous times in the Hebrew manuscripts.

If we compare יְהֹוִה (*Yehovih*) with יְהוָה (*Yehvah*) the evidence points toward the *holem,* which is the dot over the *hey* ה, as being the missing vowel. This demonstrates that the scribes knew that the name was pronounced יְהֹוָה Y^{e}hovah, but they customarily omitted the *holem* so the name could not be pronounced correctly, and to remind the reader that it should not be pronounced at all. This is an important moment. If the earliest vocalized manuscripts are correct, you have just read the holiest name in the universe. There is a passage that shows how the people of Israel treated this name in worship.

And Ezra blessed Y^{e}hovah the great Elohim. And all the people answered, "Amen, Amen!" while lifting up their hands; and they bowed low and worshiped Y^{e}hovah with their faces to the ground.

NEHEMIAH 8:6

145

Can you imagine the people of יְהֹוָה אֱלֹהֵי יִשְׂרָאֵל (Y^{e}hovah Elohim of Israel)[155] reverencing His name in this way? What about you? How will you respond to this Holy Name?

Before you make a judgment, hear me out. If this was just my pet theory, with no Hebrew manuscript evidence, then you would be completely justified in disregarding this information. But there is good news! There is *actual textual evidence* that supports the pronunciation Y^{e}hovah.

In the Leningrad Codex there are 50 examples of the name יְהֹוָה Y^{e}hovah written with the complete consonants and vowels! There is no way of knowing if these were intentional or if they were scribal "slips," but the specific number of occurrences and the places in Scripture where these *holems from heaven* are used in the name יְהֹוָה Y^{e}hovah may be revelatory. The number 50 is used in Scripture for some very important things. Some examples are 50 cubits as one of the measurements of Noah's Ark; 50 loops of gold for the curtain of the tabernacle; 50 cubits as the length of the curtain; 50 as a measurement for the Temple that Ezekiel saw; and every 50 years there is to be a jubilee in Israel. But the most important 50 to me is found in Leviticus 23 regarding the biblical holy day Shavuot/Pentecost.

> You shall count fifty days to the day after the seventh Sabbath; then you shall present a new grain offering to Y^{e}hovah.
>
> LEVITICUS 23:16

Shavuot refers to the seven Sabbaths plus one day that add up to a total of 50 days! If you have had the opportunity to read *A Prayer to Our Father: Hebrew Origins of the Lord's Prayer* you know about my testimony regarding *Shavuot*. Y^{e}hovah requested my presence in His city on the Holy Day of 50! The Torah Scroll that I received in Jerusalem opened up to this very passage about Shavuot when I asked Nehemia Gordon to read it for me. Maybe

---

[155] Yehovah Elohe Yisrael, Psalms 106:48.

this helps you understand why I am so convinced that I have been led throughout this amazing journey to learn about this name.

For all who are willing to see, in Appendix B I have listed the references for all 50 places where the name is vowel pointed as יְהֹוָה Y^ehovah. Are these vowel pointings just a coincidence? Did the scribe consciously violate the rabbinical prohibition? Did he intentionally leave enough evidence for others to be able to know the name? Maybe he was caught up in the moment based on the Scripture he was copying, and in his enthusiasm wrote the name as he knew it should be. We don't know all we would like to know about this textual revelation, but the fact is that we do have these *50 witnesses* in the Leningrad Codex to the correct pronunciation of the name יְהֹוָה Y^ehovah!

I have come up with all sorts of "coincidences" based on where the fully vowel-pointed name occurs. For example, the first time it appears is in Genesis 3:14, where the serpent is cursed, and the second time is in Genesis 9:26, where there is a blessing on Shem (*name*). Check them out and have fun speculating on why the scribe intentionally or accidentally wrote the name with all its vowels so it could be read and spoken correctly by you and me!

The Second Witness

The second textual witness is the Aleppo Codex.[156] There are fascinating stories behind both of these ancient Hebrew manuscript witnesses and I strongly encourage you to do further research about their origins. I have used the Leningrad Codex as the "working" witness for this book. However, the Aleppo Codex is the crown jewel of all Hebrew manuscripts and the Leningrad was "corrected" by comparing it to the Aleppo Codex. I have only scratched the surface in terms of studying the contents of this treasure, but what I have seen has been incredible.

---

[156] The Aleppo Codex, attributed to the scribe Aharon Ben Asher, is an ancient vocalized Hebrew manuscript. Although it is older than the Leningrad Codex, it is incomplete. The Aleppo Codex is housed at the Shrine of the Book Museum in Israel.

Known by many simply as "the Crown," the Aleppo Codex is the earliest known codex of the Hebrew Bible. Considered to be the most authoritative and accurate Masoretic biblical text, it is now treasured as one of the most important biblical manuscripts in all of Jewish history.[157]

Two years after I returned from my trip to Israel, my very good friend, the late Reggie White, traveled to Jerusalem and was able to view the original Aleppo Codex that is safely guarded in a vault. We wrote about his encounter with this ancient witness in *A Prayer To Our Father: Hebrew Origins of the Lord's Prayer*.[158] He purchased a copy of the codex for me, which I consider to be a priceless gift. When he presented the beautifully bound replica of the codex he explained that only 600 limited edition copies of this manuscript were printed in 1976. I am still amazed that I can study my own copy of this ancient witness. Even though the Aleppo Codex is not complete, it is considered to be the most accurate of all vocalized Hebrew manuscripts and is about 100 years older than the Leningrad Codex. In the significant portion checked, there were several places where the name is vowel pointed exactly like the Leningrad manuscript as יְהֹוָה Y^{e}hovah! One very important example where the full vowels are placed in the name is found in Ezekiel 28:22:

Thus says אֲדֹנָי יְהֹוָה [*Adonai* Y^{e}hovah] . . .

Here you can clearly see that the vowels of אֲדֹנָי (*Adonai*) are *not* placed into the name יְהֹוָה Y^{e}hovah. Notice that the first vowel of *Adonai* אֲ (*chatef patach* under the *aleph*) is not the same as the first vowel of Y^{e}hovah יְ (*sheva* under the *yod*). This is only one of

---

[157] Tawil, Hayim, and Bernard Schneider. *Crown of Aleppo: The Mystery of The Oldest Hebrew Bible Codex.* The Jewish Publication Society, 2010.

[158] Gordon, N. and Johnson, K. *A Prayer to Our Father: Hebrew Origins of the Lord's Prayer.* Hilkiah Press, 2009, pages 35-37.

many examples where the scribe provided the necessary information to read and pronounce the name, even when it appears next to the title *Adonai!*

By now you may be interested in seeing an example from the *two* scribes who worked together to write the Aleppo manuscript: Shlomo ben Boya'a wrote the consonants and the well-known Masorete Aharon ben Moshe ben Asher added the vowels. If you are really motivated and would like to see Ezekiel 28:22 in the manuscript, there is a website dedicated to the study of the Aleppo Codex that includes the entire document for you to read and study for yourself.[159] There is also a book I highly recommend, titled *Crown of Aleppo,* by Hayim Tawil and Bernard Schneider. Enjoy!

I have presented *two* different witnesses from *two* different scribal traditions and *two* different countries of origin (Egypt and Israel). Both of these Hebrew manuscripts have the full vocalized spelling of the name Y^{e}hovah! This is an easily-verifiable fact, not a scholarly guess.

The Karaite Scribes

As I presented this information to a number of people they questioned whether or not the Masoretic scribes actually knew the correct pronunciation of the name. At this point, I would like to quote Nehemia Gordon, a Karaite Hebrew scholar:

> One question we must consider is how the Masoretes, the medieval scribes who copied the text of Scripture and suppressed the "o" in Y^{e}hovah, could have known the true pronunciation of the name. After all, the ban on the name supposedly had been in full force since the time of Abba Saul in the 2nd century C.E. One of the things we know about the Masoretic scribes is that many of them were

---

[159] http://www.aleppocodex.org/

Karaites, including those who worked on the Aleppo Codex. We also know that there were two factions of Karaites, those who required the pronunciation of the name and those who forbade it. It is clear that the Karaite Masoretes belonged to the group that forbade the pronunciation of the name and this was why they suppressed the middle vowel of Y^{e}hovah. At the same time they heard the other Karaites pronounce the name, so they knew the proper pronunciation. The 10th century Karaite sage Kirkisani reports that the Karaites who pronounced the name were based in Persia (Khorasan). Persia had been a major Israelite center ever since the 10 Tribes were exiled to the "cities of Media" (2 Kings 17:6) and remained so until the Mongol invasion in the 13th century. Because Persia was so far from the rabbinical centers of Galilee and Babylonia, the Jews of Persia were protected from the rabbinical innovations in the Mishnah and Talmud until the 7th century C.E. It was only when the rabbis attempted to impose these innovations on the Jews of Persia in the 7th and 8th centuries that the Karaite movement rose up to ensure the preservation of the old ways. So it is not surprising that the Karaites of Persia preserved the correct pronunciation of the name from ancient times. It seems that the Masoretes suppressed the vowel "o" from the divine name to prevent the Karaites from simply reading the name as it was written. Now when these Karaites read the biblical text, they had to supply the missing vowel themselves. Some Masoretes were Rabbanites, such as those who worked on the Leningrad Codex. Their identical vocalization of the name Y^{e}hovah serves as

a second, independent witness that verifies this pronunciation.[160]

If you want more *practical* evidence of the pronunciation of
the name, I suggest that you consider the following biblical names
that have the same beginning as Y^{e}hovah: Y^{e}Ho-shaphat, Y^{e}Ho-
zabad, Y^{e}Ho-ash, Y^{e}Ho-achaz, Y^{e}Ho-natan, Y^{e}Ho-iakim, Y^{e}Ho-
yakin, Y^{e}Ho-nadab, Y^{e}Ho-yarib, Y^{e}Ho-ram, Y^{e}Ho-seph, Y^{e}Ho-
adah, Y^{e}Ho-tsadaq, Y^{e}Ho-yada, Y^{e}Ho-chanan, Y^{e}Ho-shabeat,
Y^{e}Ho-adan, and Y^{e}Ho-sheba. For a little fun, try matching the
following anglicized names with the Hebrew "Yeho- names":
Jozabad, Jehoiakim, Jehoiakin, Joram, Jehoshaphat, Jehoadah,
Jehoachaz, Jehozadak, Jehoash, Jehoshabeath, Jehoiarib, Jehoaddan,
Johnathan, Johnson, Jehonadab, Jehoiada, Jehohanan, Joseph,
Jehosheba and Jehoiada. As I said, have fun.

The Jehovah's Witnesses

Before you assume that I agree with the Jehovah's Witnesses
regarding pronunciation of the name, consider this. The English
Jehovah is an anglicized form of Y^{e}hovah. There are three major
differences between the names Y^{e}hovah and Jehovah. The first
difference is that there is no "J" sound in Hebrew. If you are
interested in why *Jesus* is not the original pronunciation of his
name, you will learn about the "late j" in the bonus chapter of this
book. The second difference is that the name Y^{e}hovah in the
Hebrew manuscripts always has the accent on the *end* of the
name—Y^{e}ho**vah**, with the emphasis on "vah." Pronouncing the
name Je**ho**vah, with the emphasis on the "ho," is an English
mispronunciation of Y^{e}hovah. The third difference is the raised *e* in
the name that focuses on the sound "ye," which is distinct from the
way some people say Jahovah. The Y^e sound comes from the *sheva*
under the *yod* (?). (When *yod* comes at the beginning of a word it is
considered a partial vowel in terms of pronunciation.) I have come

---

[160] Nehemia Gordon, "The Pronunciation of the Name," www.Karaite-Korner.org.

to appreciate the subtleties of the Hebrew language that affect pronunciation. Guttural and breathing sounds along with accents really add a special dimension to this lovely language.

Pronouncing the name Y^{e}hovah is a beautiful and meaningful act of worship that should not be trampled upon or trivialized. The name is pronounced "Y^e" with a short half vowel, "ho" just like it is spelled, and "vah" as a breath with an accent—Y^e-ho-**vah**. When you finish this book I hope you take the opportunity to learn the list of names and also use the instructional CD in Appendix A that will help you learn how to pronounce this holy, precious, and powerful name.

The Name in the King James Version

One of the most interesting discoveries regarding the name Y^{e}hovah in English translations is found in the original 1611 version of the King James Bible. I referred to this in Chapter Six. Nehemia and I also wrote about this discovery in our book *A Prayer to Our Father: Hebrew Origins of the Lord's Prayer.*[161] As we explained, there are several places in the old KJV where the translators disregarded the ban on revealing the name and actually printed it in English with the proper vowels. I have looked into my beloved grandmother Fannie Mae Hayes' old KJV family Bible and found four verses where the name is printed as JEHOVAH.[162] In three of the four places the name is printed in italics for emphasis. The fourth time it is written as IEHOVAH, just as it is pronounced in Hebrew without the anglicized letter J! You can see them for yourself on the website of the University of Pennsylvania.[163]

There you can view the full-sized image of the title page. At the very top of the page, just above the dove that represents the Holy Spirit, in small Hebrew letters, יהוה is printed with two of the

---

[161] Gordon, N. and Johnson, K. *A Prayer to Our Father: Hebrew Origins of the Lord's Prayer.* Hilkiah Press, 2009, pages 102-103.
[162] See Exodus 6:3, Psalms 83:18, Isaiah 12:2, Isaiah 26:4.
[163] http://sceti.library.upenn.edu/sceti/printedbooksnew/index.cfm?TextID=kjbible&PagePosition=139.

three vowel points (without the *holem*), representing the name of our Heavenly Father יְהֹוָה שָׁמָּה (Y^ehovah Is There).[164] His name is above all things in heaven and on earth!

I also would like to explain what you will see if you go to Exodus chapter 6 in this online version. There are *two* places in the 1611 version where the name is written in the text without the anglicized J. It is spelled out as IEHOVAH in the chapter heading and again in verse 3. Below you can see the words just as they appear in Exodus 6 in the 1611 version of the KJV.

CHAP. VI.

God renueth his promife by his name IEHOVAH.

6:3 And I appeared unto Abraham, unto Ifaac, and unto Jacob, by the Name of God Almighty, but by my name IEHOVAH was I not known to them.

It literally gave me a chill the first time I saw these *two* witnesses with my own *two* eyes. Do you understand why this is an important witness to the name יְהֹוָה Y^ehovah? In 1611 people actually had the opportunity to read and pronounce His name. In fact, even though JEHOVAH was printed with the "J" in the other three places, the name was still pronounced IEHOVAH. It was not until 23 years after the publication of the 1611 version of the Bible that a distinction was made between the letters "I" and "J."[165] If you look in the American Standard Version, printed in 1901, you will see the name JEHOVAH seven times.[166]

Even though there has been considerable criticism of the King James Version, the translators just about got it right (J vs. Y)

---

[164] Y^ehovah Shama, Ezekiel 48:35.

[165] R. Lass (editor), *The Cambridge History of the English Language.* Cambridge, 1999, volume 3, pages 28, 39.

[166] Isaiah 26:4 (three times), Isaiah 12:2 (twice), and Psalms 83:18 and Exodus 6:3 (once each).

when it came to Psalms 83:18. This verse would not, indeed does not, make sense if LORD is substituted for the name יְהֹוָה.

> That men may know that thou, whose name alone is
> JEHOVAH, art the Most High over all the earth.
>
> PSALMS 83:18 (King James Version)

You now possess the information to answer the many critics of the correct pronunciation, even though many scholarly sources still advance arguments that can be proven false by the Hebrew manuscript evidence. Here are some examples:

> *Webster's Collegiate Dictionary:* "Jehovah — False reading of the Hebrew YAHWEH." ("Jehovah," *Webster's New Collegiate Dictionary,* 1973 ed.)

> *Encyclopedia Americana:* "Jehovah — erroneous form of the name of the God of Israel." (*Encyclopedia Americana,* vol. 16, 1972 ed.)

> *Encyclopædia Britannica:* "The Masoretes who from the 6th to the 10th century worked to reproduce the original text of the Hebrew Bible replaced the vowels of the name YHWH with the vowel signs of Adonai or Elohim. Thus the artificial name Jehovah came into being." ("Yahweh," *The New Encyclopædia Britannica,* vol. 12, 1993 ed.)

> *The Jewish Encyclopedia:* "Jehovah — a mispronunciation of the Hebrew YaHWeH the name of God. The pronunciation of Jehovah is grammatically impossible." ("Jehovah," *The Jewish Encyclopedia,* vol. 7, 1904 ed.)

The New Jewish Encyclopedia: "It is clear that the word Jehovah is an artificial composite." ("Jehovah," *The New Jewish Encyclopedia,* 1962 ed.)

I hope you feel confident enough to see through the erroneous statements made in these sources. I will only accept their opinions if they explain what I am to do with the *unmistakable Hebrew manuscript evidence* for יְהֹוָה Y^ehovah.

The Wrong Tool

Now to address the somewhat popular notion that the name יְהֹוָה Y^ehovah is based on the Hebrew word meaning "disaster." The people who make this sensational but unfounded argument have used the wrong tool to dig for the truth. They usually start by offering to give the "secret" to the meaning of the name *Jehovah.*

They pull out the ever-popular reference book called *Strong's Exhaustive Concordance of the Bible.*[167] It is a wonderful tool that can help people identify the Hebrew words that are behind the English words in the KJV Bible. Even though it is based on 19th-century scholarship, this concordance is fairly reliable in many of its lexicon definitions. One of the best ways to determine the true meaning of a biblical word is to look it up in a bona fide Hebrew lexicon to see its meaning in various contexts. Also, Hebrew has verb forms, tenses, and stems that affect the meaning of words. Strong's lexicon doesn't deal with this important aspect of the Hebrew language, which is the main problem with the theory that the name Y^ehovah is derived from a word meaning "disaster." Its proponents use a helpful tool, but they create an incorrect and harmful result. I do not want to denigrate anyone's desire for truth, but the root of the argument is flawed.

The starting point is the word הֹוָה (*hovah*), which means mischief, ruin, or disaster. They give the Strong's number (H1943 or 01943) for support. Then they say the root of this Hebrew word

---

[167] Strong, J. *Strong's Exhaustive Concordance of The Bible.* Thomas Nelson Publishers, 1990.

is הַוָּה (*havah*), which means evil desire, ruin, or destruction, using Strong's number (H1942 or 01942) as further evidence. Their conclusion, based on the previous information, is that since הֹוָה (*hovah*) sounds just like a portion of *Jehovah,* the meaning of the name must really be "disaster." Some people also conclude that since Satan is the author of mischief, ruin, and disaster, he is behind the meaning of the name Jehovah. What they fail to do is look at all of the meanings of the root word הֹוָה (*hovah*), rather than just the one that appears to fit their theory. There are six other possible meanings for these three letters depending on the vowel combination, as is the case with many Hebrew words. Anyone can make a similar argument by forcing the letters or sounds to conform to a desired meaning.

The truth is that the root word of the name יְהֹוָה Y^{e}hovah is not הֹוָה (*hovah*), but הָיָה (*hayah*), which has already been explained in Chapter Seven under the section "The Answer." The name יְהֹוָה Y^{e}hovah is a proper noun that comes from the masculine verb form הָיָה (*hayah*); הֹוָה (*hovah*) is a feminine noun. The argument regarding הֹוָה (*hovah*) may sound intriguing to the untrained ear, but it is not supported by Hebrew grammar or the biblical text.

If someone has tried to convince you of this false teaching you may wish to consider adding some good Hebrew grammar resources to your biblical tool box.[168]

The name Y^{e}hovah flows out of the mouth in English just like it does in Hebrew, with beauty and ease. The vowel *holem,* which is in the middle, completes the name in *two* ways. First, it allows us to pronounce the name. Second, four consonants and three vowels make the number seven, which in the Hebrew mindset represents fulfillment and completion! Okay that is just my excitement talking, not scholarly information. I call the *holem* "the vowel point from heaven." It is the only vowel that is written above the letters; the others are written inside, below, or next to the letter. This same *"holem* from heaven" is in the words אֲדֹנָי (*Adonai*) and

---

[168] See Appendix C.

אֱלֹהִים (*Elohim*). Both of these words are used to describe the one and only יְהֹוָה Y^ehovah!

You are welcome to debate with me about the name Y^ehovah if you show me biblical or Hebrew manuscript evidence that refutes these witnesses of this Holy Name. I have read more pages of information on the name than I can count, and have been disappointed by the endless assumptions, guesses, and theories. There is no substitute for actually seeing clear evidence in the biblical text!

It is interesting to note that the Talmud acknowledges both the writing and pronunciation of this most holy and "secret" name. There is even an admission that eventually the "rabbinic ban" will be lifted and the name will again be spoken by all!

> This world is not like the world to come. In this world the name is written Yeho[vah] and read Ado[nai], but in the world to come it will be one, written Yeho[vah] and read Yeho[vah].
>
> Babylonian Talmud, Pesachim 50a

Pronunciation Possibilities

There are some reasonable arguments about the pronunciation being Y^ehowah rather than Y^ehovah. Some people contend that the *v* sound is influenced by European languages. There is no definitive way to prove either pronunciation, short of hearing a recording from the conversation that took place at the burning bush or the introduction made from Mount Sinai. This issue has to do with the ו (*vav* or *waw*), which you have learned is the third letter of the name. An example of pronouncing this letter differently would be in the name David. Those who would argue that the ו is a waw sound would call the king of Israel "Dawid."

In addition, there is clear evidence that the ancient Israelites had different pronunciations for certain words, possibly as a result of regional accents. There is a concrete example of this in Judges 12:5-6:

The Gileadites captured the fords of the Jordan opposite Ephraim. And it happened when any of the fugitives of Ephraim said, "Let me cross over," the men of Gilead would say to him, "Are you an Ephraimite?" If he said, "No," then they would say to him, "Say now, Shibboleth." But he said, "Sibboleth," for he could not pronounce it correctly. . . .

I leave room for the possibility that the name could have had more than one pronunciation. I have chosen to consistently pronounce the *vav* as a *v* sound when used in this context, as is the practice of many Jewish people today. I realize that many people prefer to use pronunciations of this holy name based on tradition, theology, or just plain trust of the one from whom they heard it. I simply want to give due consideration to what can be seen in the *two* Hebrew manuscript witnesses to which we have access. I hope this attempt to explain what I have learned about the true pronunciation of this awesome name will simply be taken as my humble desire to follow the instruction given in this psalm:

I will tell of Your name to my brethren; in the midst of the assembly I will praise You.

PSALMS 22:22

I want the people who have joined me in this study to get a valuable glimpse of the holiness of the name יְהֹוָה Y^ehovah.

There is one more biblical picture of the response to this name that I must share. The Holy Scriptures give us an amazing peek into heaven where this name is proclaimed. The prophet Isaiah describes the scene in great detail:

In the year of King Uzziah's death I saw Adonai sitting on a throne, lofty and exalted, and the train of His robe filling the temple. Seraphim stood above him, each had six wings: with two he covered his face, and with two he covered his feet, and with two he flew. And one called out to another and said, "Holy, Holy, Holy, is Y^{e}hovah of hosts, the whole earth is full of His glory." And the foundations of the thresholds trembled at the voice of him who called out, while the temple was filled with smoke.

ISAIAH 6:1–4

Can you imagine what that would sound like? Y^{e}hovah must enjoy hearing His name sung by the Heavenly Host. We have an opportunity to practice our part in the coming international choir of praise! The sound of the name Y^{e}hovah is absolute music to my ears! His name has become *"my strength and my song."*[169] Please consider joining me in practicing for this coming mass choir? Do you sing soprano, alto, tenor, or bass? With each note you sing, your strength will increase.

It is now decision time. You must decide if the Hebrew manuscripts are bona fide, worthy witnesses of the pronunciation of this powerful name. If you believe they are, then you now know the *sanctified* name of our Heavenly Father יְהֹוָה מְקַדִּשְׁכֶם (Y^{e}hovah Who Sanctifies You).[170] But if the manuscripts have not convinced you, your only alternative is to continue guessing.

If you are convinced that His name is Y^{e}hovah, and that it is supposed to be spoken, you are now able to fulfill the prayer of King David when he said to Y^{e}hovah:

... that Your name may be magnified forever, by saying, "Yehovah of hosts is Elohim over Israel" ...

2 SAMUEL 7:26

[169] Exodus 15:2.
[170] Y^{e}hovah Mikkadeshkem, Exodus 31:13 (see also Leviticus 20:8, 21:8, 22:32).

שִׁירוּ לֵאלֹהִים זַמְּרוּ שְׁמוֹ סֹלּוּ לָרֹכֵב בָּעֲרָבוֹת בְּיָהּ שְׁמוֹ

Sing to Elohim, sing praises to His name; lift up a song for him who rides in the deserts, whose name is בְּיָהּ. . . .

PSALMS 68:4

ט

TET

CHAPTER NINE

THE NAME FOR THE NATIONS

Take a moment to look at Psalms 68:4 and see how the Hebrew word בְּיָהּ (actually it is two words in English) is translated in your Bible. More than likely the title "the LORD" is used for this Hebrew word. Y^{e}hovah is actually one of *two* (of course there are *two*) forms of the personal name of our Heavenly Father witnessed in the Hebrew manuscripts. There has been no argument about the pronunciation of this second witness. It is first found in Exodus 15:2. We should not be surprised that Moses is the first one to proclaim and pronounce this powerful, poetic name. In Chapter Seven we learned that Moses, the first man who taught the name Y^{e}hovah to the Israelites, also revealed this poetic form of the name.

At first glance you might think there is no way to know that this *second* witness actually exists. The English translators have used the same "device" to hide this name as they have with Y^{e}hovah. Let's look at my ordination Bible, which happens to be the New Revised Standard Version.

Then Moses and the Israelites sang this song to the
LORD: "I will sing to the LORD, for he has triumphed
gloriously; horse and rider he has thrown into the
sea. The **LORD** is my strength and my might, and he
has become my salvation. . . . the LORD is his name."

EXODUS 15:1–3 (NRSV)

Did you catch that revelation? I made the third **LORD** bold
so you would not miss it. This verse is the first place the *second*
form of the name is used. By now you know that the English
translators concealed the name Y^{e}hovah, so we should expect them
to do the same with this *second* form of the awesome name.
However, if you look in the Hebrew Scriptures this is what you will
see when you get to the bold **LORD** in verse 2:

יָהּ

These *two* consonants and *two* vowels are the poetic form of
the name Y^{e}hovah. Notice a little dot in the middle of the ה (hey); it
is called a *mappiq* and gives a breath sound to what would normally
be a silent letter. Can you see the connection with the four-letter
name יהוה? If you take the first and second letters or the first and
last letters of that name and add the vowels it will spell יָהּ. This
form is used 49 times in Scripture exactly as you see it here. People
have spoken this name throughout the earth, and even in the midst
of the heavens, without knowing that they were speaking the poetic
version of the personal name Y^{e}hovah. You have probably heard
and even spoken this wonderful name yourself. When you look at
these Hebrew letters, do you know how to pronounce them? If not,
the New King James Version (NKJV) can help.[171]

In the New King James Version all the occurrences of

---

[171] Commissioned in 1975 by Thomas Nelson Publishers. One hundred thirty Bible scholars,
church leaders, and lay Christians worked for seven years to create a completely new,
modern translation of Scripture, which would retain the purity and stylistic beauty of the
original King James Bible.

JEHOVAH or IEHOVAH were replaced with the English title LORD. However, I was able to find four witnesses of the name that still exist even in this modern English Bible!

> Behold, God is my salvation, I will trust and not be afraid; for YAH, the LORD, is my strength and song; He has also become my salvation.[172]
>
> ISAIAH 12:2 (NKJV)

There it is. The 130 scholars who worked on the New King James Version did not feel comfortable printing the full name יְהֹוָה Y^ehovah, but when they came across the beautiful poetic form יָה Yah they rendered it properly. I wonder if the individual who suggested doing this was a member of the angelic choir who was at the translators' meeting disguised as a human. However it happened, the witness is right there for all to see.

For some reason they only chose to do this four times, even though there are 49 places where they could have included this beautiful name in our English Bible.[173] I wonder why they picked the number four (2 x 2?). It should be noted that even in the 1611 version of the KJV there is an example of *JAH* in Psalms 68:4.

On July 20, 1969, *two* men made history by walking on the surface of the moon. People from around the world saw and heard this historic event. Many remarkable things were said during this amazing trip to the moon, but the statement I want to focus on was made by the least-known man on the mission. He never left the spacecraft, so no one saw him on television during the historic landing. However, I believe what he said may have reached beyond the ears of humankind to the very throne room of יְהֹוָה יִרְאֶה (Y^ehovah Who Sees).[174] After Neil Armstrong and Edwin (Buzz) Aldrin finished walking on the moon, Michael Collins had this

---

[172] Also see Isaiah 26:4, 38:11 and Psalms 68:4 in the New King James Version. Copyright © 1982, by Thomas Nelson, Inc. Used by permission. All rights reserved.

[173] See Appendix B for the 49 Scripture references for Yah.

[174] Y^ehovah Yireh, Genesis 22:14.

exchange with Mission Control in Houston that involved the powerful poetic name יָהּ (*Yah*).

> 112:06:12 Collins: Roger, Columbia on (Omni) Charlie. How do you read?

> 112:06:16 McCandless: Roger, Columbia. This is Houston. Reading you loud and clear on Omni Charlie. The crew of Tranquility Base is back inside their base, repressurized, and they're in the process of doffing the PLSSs. Everything went beautifully. Over.

> 112:06:36 Collins: Hallelujah![175]

Michael Collins may not have been well known on earth, but when he said that word (actually two words in Hebrew) he probably became famous in heaven. He may not have walked on the moon, but he was the first man beyond the boundaries of earth to openly praise the name יָהּ יְהֹוָה (Yah Y^ehovah).[176]

This is amazing to me. When I go outside and look up at the moon and realize that it is over 220,000 miles away, I cannot help but think about Michael Collins. I hope you realize that he has the same name as one of the angels in heaven (Michael in English and מיכאל [*Mikael*] in Hebrew).[177] Michael מיכאל in Hebrew means *"who is like El."* Could this be why Michael Collins, in a moment of great excitement and relief, said these *two* Hebrew words? Was he looking at the moon and thinking that it is the great calendar in the sky? Was he looking at the earth and realizing that it had been created by words from the mouth of Elohim? Maybe he saw the bright stars against the dark backdrop of space and thought to

---

[175] *Apollo 11 Lunar Surface Journal*, www.hq.nasa.gov.

[176] Yah Y^ehovah, Isaiah 12:2.

[177] See Daniel 10:13, 10:21, 12:1 in the Tanach and Jude 9, and Revelation 12:7 in the New Testament.

himself *"who is like El"* and just said *two* words that would do honor to this amazing Being.

His response to Mission Control could have been any number of *two-word* combinations—Great job! All right! Oh yeah! Thank you! That's good! Instead, he decided to say these *two* Hebrew words *Hallelujah!* I am sure someone on this study journey is saying, *"Keith, you've gone too far with this number two issue because Hallelujah is only one word."* In English it has been made into one word, possibly to conceal the fact that, in Hebrew, these *two* words "bust the ban" on pronouncing the name. Let me give you an illustration and an explanation.

Did you notice that even though the English spelling is *Hallelujah* with a *"j,"* the Hebrew pronunciation has survived? I can imagine a young girl, when preparing for confirmation at a good United Methodist church, is asked to select a Bible passage to read in front of the congregation. I can also imagine that she selects Revelation 19:6. During dress rehearsal when she comes to the word *Hallelujah* she stops reading and with a confused look on her face asks the pastor, *"Should I pronounce the 'j' with a 'y' sound or a 'j' sound?"* The pastor tells her it is pronounced as a *"y"*. If my son Andrew is in this class, he will raise his hand and ask the pastor his famous question: *"Why?"*

Unfortunately, the pastor cannot get away with an answer like *"Tradition"* or *"Just because."* Allow me to help my fellow United Methodist clergywoman and explain to the class why the young lady should say *hallelujah* with a *"y"* sound, instead of the way it is written. Anyone who says *hallelujah is* praising the name of the Creator of heaven and earth with *two* Hebrew words, *hallelu* and *Yah* because He is הָי (*Yah*). These two words are written side by side 26 times in the Hebrew Scriptures.[178]

Hallelujah means "praise Yah." It connects הַלְלוּ (*Hallelu*) *praise* with the name הָי (*Yah*). The form *Yah* follows the ancient

---

[178] See Psalms 102:18, 104:35, 105:45, 106:1, 106:48, 111:1, 112:1, 113:1, 115:17, 115:18, 116:19, 117:2, 135:1, 135:3, 135:21, 146:1, 146:10, 147:1, 147:20, 148:1, 148:14, 149:1, 149:9, 150:1, and 150:6 *twice* in the same verse!

practice of taking the *first* and *last* letters of a word to create an abbreviation. This is also very common in Greek. For example, *KE* is a common abbreviation for *Kourie/kyrie, Lord.*[179]

There is also a statement by Theodoret of Cyrus who said, *"The Jews call Him AIA."*[180] This is the abbreviated or poetic form *Yah* with an added prosthetic *aleph.*[181] Theodoret is saying that the Jews of his time called יְהֹוָה by the name *A-Yah*.

If the same young lady from the United Methodist confirmation class had read Psalm 150 in Hebrew rather than English, her first two words would have been הַלְלוּ יָהּ (*Hallelu Yah*). English Bibles usually render these *two* Hebrew words as *Praise the* Lord. However, the translator of the Book of Revelation did not "get the memo" banning the name in the New Testament, so he wrote these *two* Hebrew words four times in the book, the only occurrences of *Hallelujah* in the entire New Testament.[182]

Even Jewish sages have acknowledged that יָהּ Yah is the abbreviated or poetic form of the personal name יְהֹוָה Y^ehovah. And even though it was not formally "banned," they have attempted to diminish its value. Here is the commentary on Exodus 15:2 by Ramban, which is an acronym for Rabbi Moshe ben Nachman. Considered one of the greatest Torah scholars of his time, he is quoted quite often in other Jewish commentaries.

> *Ramban* notes that this verse uses the abbreviated form of the Name [יָ-הּ] and the next verse uses the full Name [יְ-הֹ-וָ-הּ]. The shorter form sometimes indicates that the full degree of His greatness has been hidden from the world due to man's shortcomings.[183]

---

[179] Nehemia Gordon, "The Pronunciation of the Name," www.Karaite-Korner.org.

[180] Theodoret of Cyrus, *Quaestio 15 in Exodus: A commentary on the pronunciation of the name by the Samaritans* (in Latin).

[181] A prosthetic aleph is the Hebrew letter א (*aleph*) added to the beginning of a word to facilitate pronunciation.

[182] See Revelation 19:1, 19:3, 19:4 and 19:6.

[183] The Stone Edition Chumash, edited by Rabbi Nosson Scherman/Rabbi Meir Zlotowitz. Brooklyn, New York: Mesorah Publications, 2001, pages 376-377, paragraph 2.

Is this really the case regarding the shorter form of the name, or is it simply an attempt to perpetuate the agenda of banning it? According to Rashi (see Chapter Seven), Moses was not told to conceal this abbreviated name as he supposedly was instructed to do with the fully-spelled name. Does this really make any sense? Both יְהֹוָה and יָה are His name, and when spoken with passion, both carry the same power, privilege, and purpose. The poetic and abbreviated form יָה Yah is not short on *His greatness*. The bottom line is that the famous ban on the name is busted! It did not work. The name יְהֹוָה Y^ehovah is being revealed again!

Let's make a short visit back to my *imagined meeting in heaven* from Chapter Two. Notice again the first recorded word spoken by יְהֹוָה, which can be seen in any Hebrew Bible in Genesis 1:3 as יְהִי. Now look again at the poetic name without vowels יה (*Yah*). Read the word יהי with your right-handed brain or your newly-developed left-handed approach. What do you see? You should recognize His poetic name יה either way you read it! I hope you remember that both יְהֹוָה and יָה are related to this word יהי (*Yehee*), which comes from the verb היה (*hayah*). Now will you respond like the angels?

How creative is יְהֹוָה Y^ehovah that He would make and form words like these! He is called יְהֹוָה עֹשָׂה יְהֹוָה יוֹצֵר אוֹתָהּ (Y^ehovah Who Made It, Y^ehovah Who Formed It).[184] He could have chosen anything as the first recorded word from His mouth. What an awesome word He chose that, even when I say it, I think of Him. Can you hear Him in this word יהי *yehee*? I hear *Yea He* revealed His name again!

After completing the "beta version" of this book, I traveled to South Africa for a speaking tour with Nehemia. It was not my intention to discuss this study since it was still a work in progress. However, an encounter with one of the "many nations" inspired me to change my mind.

---

[184] Y^ehovah Osah Y^ehovah Yotzer Otah, Jeremiah 33:2. Notice the final letter ה, which is the third feminine singular meaning "it".

As we traveled in South Africa speaking and preaching about the message of our book, we had some amazing experiences. Early in our trip Nehemia came down with the African equivalent of *Montezuma's revenge*. He later called it *"Shaka Zulu's revenge."* He really was quite sick, yet his sense of humor was still intact. As he lay in bed for the day, I took advantage of the opportunity to venture out to a beautiful place called the valley of a thousand hills where I encountered a Zulu tribe that changed my entire message for the remainder of our tour.

In a land filled with such diversity of language and race, it was a challenge to find ways to bring people together in unity. There are eleven official languages in South Africa and many different ethnic groups living as neighbors in the same land. Through our relationship and message, Nehemia and I were intent on demonstrating that there can be unity in the midst of diversity. My Zulu brothers and sisters truly helped our cause!

After this tribe danced and sang in their traditional dress, there was a moment of silence; then, suddenly something happened that seemed completely out of context. One of the Zulu men shouted out praise to the name of God *in Hebrew!* After recovering from minor shock, I walked into the midst of the men and women and repeated what he said. To my amazement the entire group began singing three Hebrew words over and over that praised the name of our Heavenly Father! At that point I joined in and we had a good old-fashioned singing and dancing celebration.

After my encounter, I then used what I had learned from my Zulu brothers and sisters for the rest of our tour. I closed each session with their beautiful song that calls every language and people to unity in the Hebrew name of our Heavenly Father! Throughout South Africa there were people in our audiences who spoke a wide variety of languages and dialects, but when they sang this song they all pronounced these three Hebrew words just as the Zulus did. I felt like I had struck gold!

It was really quite a sight to see white Afrikaners sing and dance like Zulus with black Africans in a Dutch Reformed church. When a white Jewish scholar and an African-American, United

Methodist preacher were added to the mix, it really was quite a sight to see!

The three Hebrew words sung by my Zulu brothers and sisters were, *Amen* (truth), *Hallelu* (praise), and *Yah* (the poetic form of the name Y^{e}hovah that Moses introduced to the Israelites in a song!). What I find fascinating is that in my Hebrew Bible, at the end of Psalms 106:48, these three words are in the exact order as in the Zulu song!

אָמֵן הַלְלוּ יָהּ (Amen Hallelu Yah!)

This is the *only* place in the entire Hebrew Bible where they are in this order! How did these Zulu men and women learn this song with these words in this particular order? Maybe it was handed down from generations past. Who knows?

This song proclaims an amazing truth. Y^{e}hovah has not allowed any language to completely obscure the praise of this holy name! I have traveled to six continents and have been among people who speak scores of different languages. No matter what native language the people speak, these *three* Hebrew words are always spoken the same! Some people consider the words *Hallelu Yah* as the highest praise to Yah![185] Praise יְהֹוָה Y^{e}hovah, בְּיָהּ שְׁמוֹ (In Yah is His Name).[186] When you add a good old-fashioned amen, as my Zulu brothers and sisters did, these words transcend the barriers of every tongue, tribe, and nation. May it be that every person on this earth learns to bless His holy name this way!

> And blessed be His glorious name forever; and may the whole earth be filled with His glory. Amen, and Amen.
>
> PSALMS 72:19

---

[185] See Nehemiah 9:5.

[186] B'yah Shemo, Psalms 68:5 in English and 68:4 in Hebrew.

My experience with the Zulus spurred me on to look for unity in South Africa, a land of great diversity. The name answered the call! I found a name for the nations! The following three verses promote the benefits of the name:

The name יְהֹוָה is a strong tower; the righteous runs into it and is safe.

PROVERBS 18:10

Because he has loved Me, therefore I will deliver him; I will set him securely on high, because he has known My name.

PSALMS 91:14

May יְהֹוָה answer you in the day of trouble. May the name of the Elohim of Jacob exalt you.[187]

PSALMS 20:1 (Keith Johnson Version)

Knowing the name יְהֹוָה sets us securely in an exalted and safe place.

All three of the previous verses use the exact same Hebrew word, שגב (sagav), for the English expressions safe, securely on high, and exalted. South Africa and all other nations on this planet need to learn this exalted, secure and safe name; all people everywhere need to live in this name, love this name, and find refuge in the name יְהֹוָה Y^ehovah!

Now are you willing to open your mouth and give praise to Y^ehovah who is called Yah? הַלְלוּ יָהּ הַלְלוּ אֶת שֵׁם יְהֹוָה (Hallelu Yah, Hallelu the Name Y^ehovah).[188]

It is my hope that the information in this chapter will go a long way toward fulfilling my prayer to Y^ehovah according to Psalms 45:17:

---

[187] יְשַׂגֶּבְךָ (yisgavka) piel imperfect to be exalted from שגב (sagav).
[188] Psalms 135:1.

I will cause Your name to be mentioned in all generations; therefore the peoples will praise, confess, and thank You forever and ever.

PSALMS 45:17, English (Keith Johnson Version)

Below is the Hebrew text of this verse. Will you try to say it? For you brave study partners, be creative; compose your own music for this beautiful verse and sing it in Hebrew. I sing these words to the tune *Kumbayah*.

אַזְכִּירָה שִׁמְךָ בְּכָל דֹּר וָדֹר עַל כֵּן עַמִּים יְהוֹדֻךָ לְעֹלָם וָעֶד

PSALMS 45:18, Hebrew

Azkirah skeemka bechol dor vador, al ken amim yehoduka le'olam vaed.

Writing this book is my humble attempt to encourage people all over the world to praise His sanctified name. After you read the final chapter, I hope you will take advantage of the instructional CD in the back of the book so you can learn to pronounce, and yes even sing, His name!

Sing Y^{e}hovah, for He has done excellent things. Let this be known throughout the earth.

ISAIAH 12:5 (Keith Johnson Version)

171

עַתָּה אָקוּם יֹאמַר יְהֹוָה עַתָּה אֵרוֹמָם עַתָּה אֶנָּשֵׂא

"Now I will arise," says Y^ehovah, "Now I will be exalted, now I will be lifted up."

ISAIAH 33:10

י

YOD

CHAPTER TEN

A CALL TO ACTION

You are now ready to visit the mountainside in Israel where the famous prayer to *our Father who art in heaven* was taught to the Jewish multitude. The first word of this prayer in Hebrew is *Avinu,* which means "Our Father."

If *Jesus*[189] had been confronted by a rabbi and asked to show from the Scriptures why Y^ehovah should be called *our Father,* he might well have opened a scroll to Isaiah 63:16. If you were able to look over his shoulder as he read, you might recognize *two* of the Hebrew words in the scroll. Here is the relevant phrase from the passage in Isaiah:

אתה יהוה אבינו

It says, *"You Y^ehovah are our Father."* This is just one of several verses that declare His name, followed immediately by a

---

[189] I have italicized the name *Jesus* in this chapter for emphasis. It is my hope that you will read the bonus chapter "What About the Name *Jesus?*" in order to learn his original Hebrew name.

description of His relationship to His people. *Jesus* knew that יְהֹוָה Y^ehovah is our Heavenly Father!

He also knew the many passages that proclaim the name יְהֹוָה as holy. Psalms 145:21 says, *"My mouth will speak the praise of Y^ehovah, and all flesh will bless his holy name forever and ever."* He certainly must have read Psalms 103:1, which says, *"Bless Y^ehovah, O my soul, and all that is within me, bless His holy name."* There is no question that he had heard and even studied Psalms 105:3, that says, *"Glory in His holy name; let the heart of those who seek Y^ehovah be glad!"* He no doubt felt confident teaching the people to sanctify the name because of what he read in Exodus 31:13: *"You shall surely observe My Sabbaths; for this is a sign between Me and you throughout your generations, I am Y^ehovah Mikaddishkem [Who Sanctifies you]."* Finally, *Jesus* undoubtedly knew the name and description that יְהֹוָה Y^ehovah gave Himself: יְהֹוָה קדוש בישראל (*Y^ehovah Holy in Israel*).[190]

Is this why *Jesus* spoke a unique prayer that combines *two* words that are not used together anywhere else in the Tanach or the New Testament? His prayer is instructive for those of us who desire to *sanctify* the name of our Heavenly Father יְהֹוָה Y^ehovah. These first *two* words are revelatory when used together in prayer.

> Holy Father, keep them in Your name. . . .
>
> JOHN 17:11

The word *holy* in Greek is αγιος (*agios*); it is equivalent to קדוש (*kadosh*) in Hebrew. Both words mean *to sanctify* or *set apart*. The holiness of the Father is a state of being, not a process. This is why we as His people are charged numerous times in Scripture to be holy.[191] When *Jesus* taught the people to sanctify the name of his Holy Father he must have referred to the book of Leviticus, which speaks of the holiness of Y^ehovah more than any other in the entire Bible. For example:

---

[190] Y^ehovah Kadosh b'Israel, Ezekiel 39:7.
[191] See Exodus 22:31, Leviticus 11:45, 19:2, 20:7, 21:8, Numbers 15:40.

> Thus you are to be holy [קדשים, *kadoshim*] to Me, for
> I יְהֹוָה am holy [קדוש, *kadosh*]; and I have set you
> apart from the peoples to be Mine.
>
> LEVITICUS 20:26

The word קדוש (*kadosh*) is the basis for *sanctifying* the name of our Heavenly Father. In John 17:11 *Jesus* is asking his Holy Father to guard or keep us in the holy name יְהֹוָה Y^{e}hovah.

He was guided by the scriptural proclamations and the revelation of the name יְהֹוָה Y^{e}hovah as he taught the people to pray, *"Our Father in heaven your name be sanctified* [קדשים, *kadoshim*]."* He knew this was a *two*-way call to action. *Jesus* was fully aware of what would happen when the people *sanctified* the name יְהֹוָה Y^{e}hovah. He also was aware that Y^{e}hovah would act for the *sake* of His name when he heard those prayers from the sincere hearts and mouths of His people. This important phrase in this incredible prayer was not a polite, poetic, or passive acknowledgement of the *sanctified* name of his Heavenly Father. On the contrary, *Jesus* was teaching the people to pray, with purpose, the most important name in the entire universe. When he prayed, *"Your name be sanctified* [יתקדש שמך],"[192] it was a powerful proclamation of the promises that he knew were available for all who desired to pursue and pray the precious and purpose-filled name יְהֹוָה Y^{e}hovah.

Now we can look at this action-packed phrase, *"Your name be sanctified,"* from the perspective of both those who *sanctify* His name and Y^{e}hovah who performs acts for the *sake* of His name!

For His Name's Sake

The English word *sake* is based on the Hebrew word למען (*lema'an*), which is only used with a preposition and means "purpose or intent." It can be translated as *for the sake of, on*

---

[192] Yitkadesh Sheemka, in Hebrew Matthew 6:9.

account of, to the intent, or *in order that.*[193] This means that when יְהוָה Y*e*hovah acts for the sake of His name, He does it with a clear purpose. He maintains His reputation and shows His character by acting for the sake (לְמַעַן) of His name. Everything that we have learned about יְהוָה Y*e*hovah, even though it has a direct impact on us, is ultimately for His name's sake.

Let's look at the same Scriptures that *Jesus* looked at and understood regarding what יְהוָה Y*e*hovah says about His name's sake.

> For יְהוָה will not abandon his people on account of His great name, because יְהוָה has been pleased to make you a people for Himself.
>
> 1 SAMUEL 12:22

This verse teaches that יְהוָה Y*e*hovah has a reputation to uphold. His name carries covenant promises and a commitment to His people Israel.

I am sure some will ask, *"What about those of us who do not consider ourselves the people of Israel? Do we have an inheritance in this same awesome, covenant-carrying name?"*

> Also concerning the foreigner who is not from Your people Israel, when he comes from a far country for Your great name's sake and Your mighty hand and Your outstretched arm, when they come and pray toward this house, then hear from heaven, from Your dwelling place, and do according to all for which the foreigner calls to You, in order that all the peoples of the earth may know Your name, and fear [reverence] You as do Your people Israel.
>
> 2 CHRONICLES 6:32–33

---

[193] Francis Brown, *The New Brown-Driver-Briggs-Gesenius Hebrew and English Lexicon*, page 775.

At the dedication of the Temple on Mount Zion, near where I was sitting when I learned the name יְהֹוָה Yᵉhovah, Solomon prayed not only for the people of Israel, but also for everyone who would come from faraway places for the sake of His great name. I consider myself to be one of those included in Solomon's prayer.

Many promises are fulfilled *"for the sake of His name."* The following passages are just a few examples of what is done for us *"on account of"* the name יְהֹוָה Yᵉhovah.

> For Your name's sake, O יְהֹוָה, pardon my iniquity, for it is great.
>
> PSALMS 25:11

> For You are my rock and my fortress; for Your name's sake You will lead me and guide me.
>
> PSALMS 31:3

> Help us, O Elohim of our salvation, for the glory of Your name; and deliver us and forgive our sins for Your name's sake.
>
> PSALMS 79:9

> For the sake of Your name, O יְהֹוָה, revive me. In Your righteousness bring my soul out of trouble.
>
> PSALMS 143:11

Do you need forgiveness, guidance, deliverance, or revival? Even if you don't, maybe the preceding verses will be reason enough to want to know His name.

For Our Sake

Now for those who are inspired and willing to apply this information in their lives, I want to recommend three steps that can start you on the journey of *sanctifying* the name יְהֹוָה Yᵉhovah and also answer the question *"Now what?"*

The first step is to pray. Prayer is the key that unlocks the door. Barriers have been erected that have kept us from the safety this name provides. We must use prayer to tear down those barriers in our hearts and minds. You may have to deal with internal, and sometimes external, voices that try to discourage you. If you apply the information you have learned, then you might as well consider yourself in a war. But the great news is that the battle is not yours. You just need to be willing to enter the fight. May the prayer of Solomon encourage you as you continue this exciting journey:

> When Your people go out to battle against their enemy . . . and they pray to Y^{e}hovah toward the city which You have chosen and the house which I have built for Your name, then hear in heaven their prayer and their supplication, and maintain their cause.
>
> 1 KINGS 8:44–45

The second step is to practice. There are some wonderful ways to practice calling on this name. In the Scriptures there are specific references to the name Y^{e}hovah being connected to other meaningful and powerful words, just like the titles you have been learning throughout this book. As you apply these names you will begin to see some amazing things in your life. Most of these names have come from testimonies of people in the Bible who saw Y^{e}hovah in action. Appendix A lists many of these descriptive words connected to the name יְהֹוָה. If you study these powerful names you may be surprised by how practical they can become in your everyday life as you walk in the powerful name Y^{e}hovah!

The third step is to proclaim His name. Even after I had come to understand the powerful, personal name of the Creator, I did not feel I could begin speaking it freely. It seemed unfair to proclaim this awesome name in front of others if I could not give a full explanation about it. You now have an opportunity to do what took me a very long time to accomplish. You can proclaim the name יְהֹוָה Y^{e}hovah with confidence and give others the same chance to learn this life-changing information. You can become one who proclaims this name to those who need blessings, boldness, confidence, courage, deliverance, healing, peace, power, salvation, security, strength, and much more. Share what you have learned about the most important name in the entire universe with someone you love.

An instructional CD is included in the back of this book. It has a sampling of the many Hebrew descriptions and titles of יְהֹוָה Y^{e}hovah for your personal study and enjoyment as you proclaim His name. The CD will help you learn to pronounce these powerful Hebrew descriptions and names, while also teaching you a little "left-handed language." As you become comfortable with the pronunciation, these words will flow out of your mouth with beauty and power. Enjoy!

Now a word of caution. To sanctify means *to set apart as holy.* We must treat these names with reverence and respect. I adjure you to approach this most holy name יְהֹוָה Y^{e}hovah with humility, respect, honor, and reverence so it can truly be praised.

> For thus says the high and exalted One, who lives forever, whose name is holy. . . .
>
> ISAIAH 57:15

> Let them praise Your great and awesome name; holy is He.
>
> PSALMS 99:3

There is a sobering passage in Isaiah regarding those who knew and used the name, but not in truth or righteousness:

> Hear this, O house of Jacob, who are named Israel and who came forth from the loins of Judah, who swear by the name Y^{e}hovah and invoke the Elohim of Israel, not in truth nor in righteousness. For they call themselves after the holy city and lean on the Elohim of Israel; Y^{e}hovah of Hosts is His name.
>
> ISAIAH 48:1–2

I encourage you to read the rest of Isaiah 48 for yourself. Knowing and mentioning the name is only the beginning. It must become our mission to give honor to the name through our very lives! May it be so, my humble and willing study partner!

A Modern-Day Miracle

When I traveled to Israel in 2002, I witnessed a modern-day miracle that encourages me in the mission of reclaiming and proclaiming the name Y^{e}hovah. Jews who return to live in Israel are encouraged to learn the language of the land: Hebrew. I met Jews from many places around the world, including Africa, Asia, Russia, South America, and Europe. They were all speaking one language: Hebrew. The following true story about a man on a mission is the reason for my experience in Israel.

> It was about eighty years ago that a young man was inspired with a vision that Hebrew could once again live as a spoken language. His name was Eliezer ben Yehudah. He went to work and write in Israel. At first he was thought an idle dreamer, but slowly and surely, something of the fire that burned within him spread to his friends and neighbors, and to wider and wider circles, until in a few years almost all Jews in Israel were speaking Hebrew. One of the greatest miracles of all modern times had come to pass. This was the very first time in all human history that a language which ceased being spoken in ancient times came back to life on the lips of men and women and little children.[194]

Sometimes I think I must be a little like Eliezer ben Yehudah when it comes to my desire to teach people the original

---

[194] Edward Horowitz, *How The Hebrew Language Grew*, page 6. Eliezer ben Yehudah lived from 1858 to 1922.

Hebrew name יְהֹוָה. This book is the first step in fulfilling my desire. The following psalm encourages me in my quest.

Before you read the psalm, look again at the name יְהֹוָה on the cover of this book. Run your finger over the fiery four Hebrew letters. Now with His name in your mind and on your heart recite the following Scripture out loud:

> Praise יָהּ [Yah]! Praise יְהֹוָה [Y^{e}hovah] from the heavens; praise Him in the heights! Praise Him, all His angels; praise Him, all his hosts! Praise Him, sun and moon; praise Him, all stars of light! Praise Him, highest heavens, and the waters that are above the heavens! Let them praise the name יְהֹוָה [Y^{e}hovah] for He commanded and they were created. . . . Praise יְהֹוָה [Y^{e}hovah]! Praise יְהֹוָה [Y^{e}hovah] from the earth, sea monsters and all deeps; fire and hail, snow and clouds; stormy wind, fulfilling His word; mountains and all hills; fruit trees and all cedars; beasts and all cattle; creeping things and winged fowl; kings of the earth and all peoples; princes and all judges of the earth; both young men and virgins; old men and children. Let them praise the name יְהֹוָה [Y^{e}hovah], for His name alone is exalted; His glory is above earth and heaven.
>
> PSALMS 148:1–5, 7–13

I think that covers just about the whole creation. Everyone should praise the names Yah and Y^{e}hovah. What do you think? Does this passage in Scripture include you? When the name יְהֹוָה Y^{e}hovah was revealed to me I could not contain my conviction and my call to share this name. Every single one of us is included in this scriptural command to praise His name.

Now that this book has been published I must admit that I expect some opposition from those who are uncomfortable with what I have presented. In light of those impending "conversations," I have been encouraged by a gift that Nehemia Gordon, my friend and study partner, gave me. He did not realize the significance and timing of his gift, nor how it truly encouraged me to complete the task of finishing this book. He brought several of these gifts from Israel to give to the hosts who arranged our speaking engagements for our book tour in February 2010. He also offered me one. As we were preparing for our first speaking engagement in Canada he pulled out a bag of rocks. He explained that he had recently traveled to the Valley of Elah in Israel, and that he had collected these special stones from the very place where the famous battle of David and Goliath took place.

Nehemia told me that he had been looking for the spot where Scripture says David picked up five smooth stones. He eventually found an area that matched the biblical description. He asked me for my Hebrew Tanach and he turned to 1 Samuel 17 and began to read, translating directly from Hebrew. As he continued to read, his voice grew louder. Nehemia was getting quite worked up as he came to the section that said:

> Then David said to the Philistine, "You come to me with a sword, a spear, and a javelin, but I come to you in the name Y^{e}hovah of hosts, the Elohim of the armies of Israel, whom you have taunted."
>
> 1 SAMUEL 17:45

As Nehemia read this familiar story, something seemed fresh to me as he translated directly from my Hebrew Tanach. I realized that I have been facing what seems like Goliath, who at times taunts me with the weapons of history, tradition, and translation. However, I have been given a powerful gift—a stone of knowledge and experience—that continues to be smoothed by time and study.

As Nehemia continued to read, the following verse caused him to stop and take note of a rare spelling of a Hebrew word right next to the name Y^{e}hovah. I really love Hebrew! Here is what he saw:

> And all this assembly may know that not by sword or
> by spear Yehovah will cause salvation and deliverance
> [יְהוֹשִׁיעַ, *yehoshia*]. . . .
>
> 1 SAMUEL 17:47 (Keith Johnson Version)

The word that was spelled differently only occurs *two* times in the Tanach.[195] It is יְהוֹשִׁיעַ (*yehoshia*), which is best translated "he will cause to deliver/save." This rare full spelling matches the beginning pronunciation of the name Yehovah. When Nehemia was reading, the powerful word with its rare spelling and pronunciation jumped off the page, proclaiming that יְהֹוָה Yehovah will cause deliverance (יְהוֹשִׁיעַ, *yehoshia*)! I could not wait to see and study the Hebrew word for myself. In fact, it is my hope that I have transferred this same desire to you in terms of studying the Scriptures on this topic. Even in the face of all the bias and challenges, I hope you have the desire to continue to study the available information about His sanctified name!

I consider *His Hallowed Name Revealed Again* my smooth stone to hurl toward the Goliaths who taunt me about Yehovah, the Elohim of Israel. It is my continual prayer that this information will help you experience the confidence David had so you can face the Goliaths in your life with strength and assurance. In the end, it is the great and powerful name Yehovah that will *cause* us all to experience deliverance. He will give us the strength!

> For Yehovah—His eyes go to and fro in all the earth,
> to cause strength for a people whose heart is com-
> plete towards Him. . . .
>
> 2 CHRONICLES 16:9 (Keith Johnson Version)

By My Name

Now let's revisit the discussion from Chapter Three regarding Exodus 6:3:

---

[195] Also see יְהוֹשִׁיעַ in Psalms 116:6.

> I am יְהֹוָה; and I appeared to Abraham, Isaac, and Jacob, as El Shaddai,[196] but by My name, יְהֹוָה, I did not make Myself known to them.
>
> EXODUS 6:3

After taking a closer look at the words that are translated "make myself known," I noticed something that was worth slowing down to take a *second* look. The verb that is translated as "make myself known" is נוֹדַעְתִּי (*nodati*),[197] which is a verb with a suffix. This exact same form of the verb is found only four times in the entire Hebrew Bible and refers exclusively to Y^ehovah making Himself known through action!

> But I acted for the sake of My name, that it should not be profaned in the sight of the nations among whom they lived, in whose sight I made Myself known [נוֹדַעְתִּי, *nodati*] to them by bringing them out of the land of Egypt.
>
> EZEKIEL 20:9

He made Himself known to His people by the powerful feat of bringing them out of Egypt!

> "Therefore as I live," declares Adonai Y^ehovah, "I will deal with you according to your anger and according to your envy which you showed because of your hatred against them; so I will make Myself known [נוֹדַעְתִּי, *nodati*] among them when I judge you.
>
> EZEKIEL 35:11

Through judgment He made Himself known to those who were wicked toward His people.

---

[196] El Almighty, literally means El of my breasts, Exodus 6:3.

[197] This verb is a *niphal* perfect 1 common singular from the verb "to know."

It seems that when the verb נוֹדַעְתִּי (*nodati*) is used in this particular form there is an expectation that action by Y^ehovah will follow! This is what He meant when He spoke to Moses saying, "But by my name, יְהֹוָה [Y^ehovah], I did not make Myself known to them." He had revealed Himself to the patriarchs in amazing ways, but by His name Y^ehovah—with the action that follows—He had not revealed Himself. This is exactly what He is doing for us by making Himself known by His name now!

Lest you think my efforts or your willingness to apply this information will determine whether or not Y^ehovah (whose poetic name is Yah) receives praise, I would like to offer another verse as a humble reminder of the invitation to R.S.V.P. to His worldwide praise party:

> I will magnify Myself, sanctify Myself, and make Myself known [נוֹדַעְתִּי, *nodati*] in the sight of many nations; and they will know that I am Y^ehovah.
>
> EZEKIEL 38:23

Through His mighty acts He will make Himself known to the nations so all humanity will know that His name is Y^ehovah.

A Sign in the Heavens

The beta version of this study had a cover photo that illustrated the massive creative power of יְהֹוָה Y^ehovah. Although neither the picture nor my explanation can adequately portray His magnificent power and glory, I would like to try.

In July 1999 the most powerful x-ray telescope in history began its orbit thousands of miles above the earth. Ten years later, on April 3, 2009, around the time of Passover, the Chandra X-Ray Observatory sent back an image that gave a tiny glimpse of the awesome wonder and creative power of יְהֹוָה.

Approximately 17,000 light years away from earth something happened that painted a beautiful picture. A massive star ran out of fuel and collapsed, forming a pulsar, which is a rapidly spinning neutron star. This powerful pulsar was named PSR B1509-58, or simply B1509. This small, dense object, only 12 miles in diameter, was responsible for creating a remarkably large, complex, expanding nebula. The energy from this nebula made B1509 "one of the most powerful electromagnetic generators in the Galaxy," said NASA, "with a magnetic field at its surface that's 15 trillion times stronger than that of earth's."

This amazing cosmic phenomenon now spans the distance of 150 light years—hundreds of trillions of miles! Now we are able to witness this marvelous sight, which looks like a gigantic hand. In fact, when I obtained the rights from NASA to use the photograph, it was being promoted as *"the hand of God,"*[198] not literally, of course, but because of its shape. However, the timing of the arrival of this amazing picture has caused me to wonder about its purpose.

> That all the people of the earth may know that the hand of יְהֹוָה is mighty, so that you may fear [revere] יְהֹוָה your Elohim forever!
>
> JOSHUA 4:24

I have reason to believe that this cosmic event, which we are now able to see, may be a witness of what is happening in our time. It has taken almost 1,900 years for us to get to the place where the four small, but powerful, Hebrew letters of His name can finally be revealed *again* for His people to know and proclaim. These four letters represent the name יְהֹוָה—and יָהּ as a poetic abbreviation—clearly witnessed in both the Leningrad Codex B19A and the Aleppo Codex housed in Israel. The massive religious establishments are beginning to collapse and people will soon realize they need a more personal relationship with our Heavenly Father. These four letters, with the accompanying vowels that allow us to speak, sing, pray, and proclaim His personal and powerful name, are accomplishing some amazing things among His people.

---

[198] You can view this remarkable image at
http://www.nasa.gov/multimedia/imagegallery/image_feature_1323.html.

The four Hebrew letters of His name represent the One who can hold something as large as the ever-expanding universe and as small as you and me in His massive, yet tender, hands. Since He is willing to reveal His name, I decided I wanted to know it. What about you?

> Thus says יְהֹוָה who gives the sun for light by day and the fixed order of the moon and stars for light by night. . . . . יְהֹוָה of hosts is His name.
>
> JEREMIAH 31:35

The wonders appearing in the heavens, while יְהֹוָה Y^{e}hovah is revealing His name on earth, provide a witness for all who are ready to encounter the most powerful, precious, and purpose-filled name of all time!

> The heavens are telling of the glory of El; and their expanse is declaring the work of His hands.
>
> PSALMS 19:1

Y^{e}hovah is amazing, awesome, marvelous, magnificent, uncontainable, uncontrollable, living, loving, and creative, and through His name He is available to all mankind!

Mission Accomplished

My experiment of using Hebrew descriptions and names rather than the English word *God* has been a success! I found so many powerful variations of His name that I could not incorporate all of them into this book. One name I want to add here is found in the book of Psalms. My prayer has been that somehow I could complete this work that has concerned me for so long. Now that this book is in your hands, just know that you are reading something that in my humble opinion and by His grace has been completed through the One called יְהֹוָה יגמר בעדי (Y^{e}hovah Who

Shall Complete Through Me!).[199] The following verse explains the way I feel about how He has dealt with me throughout this process of learning and revealing His name:

> יְהֹוָה who completes through me.[200] Your loving-kindness, O יְהֹוָה is everlasting; do not forsake the works of your hands.

> PSALMS 138:8 (Keith Johnson Version)

The *Second* Meeting in Heaven

It is my prayer that the proclamation and praise of the name Yᵉhovah will become so prominent among His people on earth, that the following meeting will be announced in heaven: *"All the host of heaven are invited to a meeting in the throne room at the time of the sighting of the new moon regarding the revival that is taking place on earth. Please R.S.V.P. to Gabriel's office."*

Imagine the buzz that would be created among the angels if such an announcement were made. In the meeting one of the angels would raise a hand, bow his head, and ask our Heavenly Father יְהֹוָה something like, *"O Yᵉhovah Most High and Glorious, Omnipotent, Omniscient, and Omnipresent Creator of all that was, is, and ever shall be, what caused this revival on earth that has reached us in heaven?"* After silence that perhaps would seem like an eternity, the answer would come forth in words that would sound like thunder combined with rushing waters: *"There is a revival on earth because My sanctified name is being revealed again from heaven."* I am convinced that right then some angels would begin cheering and clapping; others would bow down in worship; and some would shout, "Amen! Amen!" The angelic choir would probably begin singing, *"Holy, Holy, Holy, is Yᵉhovah of hosts, the whole earth is full of His glory,"* as described in Isaiah 6:3.

---

[199] Yehovah Yigmor Ba'adee, Psalms 138:8.

[200] יִגְמֹר בַּעֲדִי Qal imperfect followed by preposition meaning to end or complete through, with one common singular suffix "me."

But wait a minute. What is your response? Are you willing to join me as we call on His holy name?

> For then I will give to the peoples purified lips, that all of them may call upon the name Y^ehovah, to serve him shoulder to shoulder.
>
> ZEPHANIAH 3:9

You probably want to know about the context of this verse before you agree to join me as an ambassador of His name. Before you answer, it is worth slowing down to take a closer look at the fiery verse before the verse above. It is connected to one of those sections in Scripture that some people like to read through quickly or skip altogether because of its difficult message and strong imagery:

> "Therefore wait for me," declares יהוה, "for the day when I rise up as a witness. Indeed my decision is to gather nations, to assemble kingdoms, to pour out on them My indignation, all my burning anger; for all the earth will be devoured by the fire of My zeal.
>
> ZEPHANIAH 3:8

I think you will agree that a verse like this is difficult to read, unless we use our left-handed Hebrew version; then we see something absolutely incredible. When I opened my Hebrew Bible this is what I saw.

All 22 Hebrew letters and the five final forms, as well as every Hebrew vowel sound, are also included in this one verse. When *two* friends from Israel told me about this, I did not accept their grand claim. I did what I hope you have done throughout this book. I checked it for myself! I suggest you find access to the Hebrew letters and vowels so you can verify what I am showing you. It really is an amazing exercise. Here it is in Hebrew if you are willing to slow down, turn aside, and see it with your own *two* eyes:

לָכֵן חַכּוּ־לִי נְאֻם־יְהוָה לְיוֹם קוּמִי
לְעַד כִּי מִשְׁפָּטִי לֶאֱסֹף גּוֹיִם לְקָבְצִי מַמְלָכוֹת
לִשְׁפֹּךְ עֲלֵיהֶם זַעְמִי כֹּל חֲרוֹן אַפִּי כִּי בְּאֵשׁ קִנְאָתִי
תֵּאָכֵל כָּל־הָאָרֶץ

ZEPHANIAH 3:8

Could it be that Zephaniah 3:8 is a witness to the importance of both the consonants and vowels of the Hebrew language? Is it possible that Y⁰hovah is revealing His name again as a witness for His remnant people in preparation for the coming redemption? After pondering these *two* questions, I looked at the verse again. I was more encouraged and less willing to rush through it or gloss over what it is saying. It also made me pause to take a *second* look at Zephaniah 3:9 and translate it directly from Hebrew:

Then I will flip [אֶהְפֹּךְ, 'ehpoke] the people's purified lip [שָׂפָה, safa] so that all of them are able to call upon the name Y⁰hovah [יְהוָה] to serve him with one shoulder.

ZEPHANIAH 3:9 (Keith Johnson Version)

After Y⁰hovah pours out His burning anger and consuming fire, He will then purify His remnant people by "flipping their lip," that is, by purifying their language so they can truly call upon His name.

Will you consider *again* my request to join me as an ambassador of His name? Here is an abbreviated account of the response of the prophet Isaiah after he saw a vision of Y⁰hovah in His throne room and the angels praising His name:

Then I said, "Woe is me, for . . . I am a man of unclean lips, and I live among a people of unclean lips. . . ." Then one of the seraphim flew to me with a burning coal in his hand. . . . He touched my mouth with it and said, "Behold, this has touched your lips. . . ." Then I heard the voice of Y⁰hovah, saying,

"Whom shall I send, and who will go for Us?" Then I said, "Here am I. Send me!"

Now that you have read Isaiah's testimony, maybe you would consider saying a prayer for purification and proclaim your willingness to be His ambassador. Be brave and say, *"Heavenly Father, please begin the purifying process now, in preparation for what is coming later."* Okay, let's go back to the scenario in heaven!

I imagine that in the midst of the smoke that would fill the temple, the sound of the doorposts shaking, all the praise and glory that would fill the meeting room, the One who is often called יְהֹוָה אֱלֹהֵי צְבָאוֹת (Y^{e}hovah Elohim of Hosts)[201] would rise from His majestic throne and quiet the Hosts of Heaven. I can imagine Him saying something like, *"Now that my people know My Holy Name,*[202] *I am ready to fill the earth with my glory. Gabriel, get my chariots of fire ready and bring your shofar."* After a statement like this, such a celebration in heaven would surely reach the eyes and ears of everyone on earth who is eagerly awaiting His arrival. When יְהֹוָה Y^{e}hovah comes to earth it will mean the restoration of all things. Are you ready?

The warmth from the fire of His name is beginning to spread all over the world. Are you willing to let it consume you? Either way, His name is coming to friend and foe alike. Ready or not here it comes:

As fire kindles the brushwood, as fire causes water to boil—to make Your name known to Your adversaries, that the nations may tremble at Your presence!

I pray that this study of His name ignites a spark in you that will start a fire that spreads from person to person, house to house,

---

[201] Yehovah Elohe Tsavaoat, Psalms 89:8 English, 89:9 Hebrew.
[202] Ezekiel 39:7.

congregation to congregation, city to city, and country to country until the whole world is full of the knowledge of His glorious name so that heaven takes notice!

> Then Y^{e}hovah will become king of the whole world.
> When that day comes, Y^{e}hovah will be the one and
> only and His name the one name.
>
> ZECHARIAH 14:9 (New Jerusalem Bible)

Now that His name has been revealed again, I want to close this book the way that יְהֹוָה Y^{e}hovah commanded the priests to bless His people by proclaiming His name. Do you remember the verse that was found on the *two* silver scrolls in Jerusalem?

> יְהֹוָה bless you, and keep you; יְהֹוָה make his face shine on you, and be gracious to you; יְהֹוָה lift up his face to you, and give you peace. So they shall invoke My name on the sons of Israel, and I will bless them.
>
> NUMBERS 6:24–27

I am יְהֹוָה, that is My name.

> ISAIAH 42:8

Bonus Chapter

WHAT ABOUT THE NAME *JESUS?*

The name *Jesus* is often the answer to a myriad of questions that Sunday school teachers ask children to elicit familiar responses and then give gobs of candy as a reward. You know how it goes: *"Who was born in a manger? Jesus! Who turned water into wine? Jesus! Who walked on water? Jesus! Who healed the blind man? Jesus! Who raised Lazarus from the dead? Jesus! Who loves you? Jesus!"* Unfortunately if those same children were asked these two questions, *"Who is Jesus named after?"* and *"What does the name* Jesus *mean?"* their little faces would draw a blank and the candy would stop flowing.

Before I go further, I realize that *Jesus* is a name that is near and dear to the hearts of many people of faith of all ages. I want you to know that it is okay if by the end of this chapter you are still completely comfortable calling him by this English name. My goal is for you to at least know the origins, meaning, and pronunciation of his name. My concern is that many Christians cannot answer the *two* questions I would ask if I were the Sunday school teacher, *"Who is Jesus named after?"* and *"What does the name* Jesus *mean?"*

This has become a problem, not only in the minds of children and adults, but also in our English Bibles. Bible translators wanted to separate the name *Jesus* from the Hebrew original, so most Christians have missed the opportunity to understand the significance and meaning of his name. You do realize that *Jesus* was Jewish and was given a Hebrew name, right? Just checking.

Because of the people I hope to reach with this book, I am not going to go into any depth regarding the many theories about the origin of the name *Jesus* outside of the Bible. You can find people who will say that the name refers to Zeus (Je'zeus) or other pagan deities.[203] There are actually *two* references to people worshipping Zeus in the New Testament.[204] Some writers even go so far as to say that the name *Jesus* has been used as a tool to Hellenize the church by the spirit of Antiochus IV Epiphanes. I have chosen to leave those theories to others; I want to focus on the actual linguistic evidence.

We know that the English name *Jesus* does cause a historical and linguistic division between Jews and Christians, as it should. What did I say? Did I say the name Jesus *should* cause division? If you ask some Jews what the name *Jesus* brings to mind, they will mention the historical atrocities committed by those who claimed allegiance to the name *Jesus*. The Spanish Inquisition and the Holocaust are only two of the many horrific examples of persecution carried out under the auspices of Christianity. This is not unlike what happened to the first African slaves that arrived in America. They were forcibly baptized *"in the name of Jesus"* as they were loaded onto *The Good Ship Jesus*.[205] The point is that many people and movements throughout history have used the name *Jesus* as a tool to justify their persecution of people.

The other issue with this English name is that *Jesus* just does not fit the language and culture of the first century. Did I say *Jesus* is an English or a Hebrew name? Why is it that our Jewish brothers and sisters do not, for the most part, even want to discuss the name *Jesus?* As hard as this may be to hear, there are probably more Jews who know about the origin of the name *Jesus* than the majority of Christians. In discussing the name יְהֹוָה Y^{e}hovah I have explained that there was a dual challenge: *tradition* and *translation*.

---

[203] Koster, C.J. *Come Out of Her, My People*. Northriding, South Africa: Institute for Scripture Research, 1998, pages 60–68.

[204] See Acts 14:12 and 14:13.

[205] Sir John Hawkins had the dubious distinction of becoming the first slave-ship captain to bring Africans to the Americas. Hawkins was a religious gentleman who insisted that his crew "serve God daily" and "love one another." His ship, ironically called *The Good Ship Jesus,* left the shores of his native England for Africa in October 1562. He arrived at Sierra Leone and in a short time he had 300 blacks in his possession. Hawkins claimed to have acquired them "partly by sword and partly by other means." Davidson, Basil, *The African Slave Trade* (Boston: Little, Brown, 1980), page 28.

Regarding the name *Jesus,* there is one word that best describes the challenge to discover his original name: *trickery.* In order to wade through this chapter you might want to put on some boots.

Where does the division enter the picture? Jews are still looking for the Messiah, and Christians say he has already come. When Jews ask the same question that Moses was asked about the name of the one who would be the deliverer, Christians say, *"His name is Jesus!"* On the other hand, Jews with even the slightest biblical knowledge know that the name *Jesus* cannot be the name of the Messiah, and they are absolutely right! How can a Hebrew Messiah come from a Hebrew family in the line of the Hebrew King David, from the Israelite tribe of Judah, and be given a name by יְהֹוָה Y^{e}hovah of the Hebrews that is derived from a *Greek* name? It makes no sense. Yet when it comes to the name *Jesus* the Christian Church continues the *translation tradition of trickery.* Now before you make any quick judgments, please hear me out.

Don't you want to learn how we have been *tricked* into being so tied to an English name translated from Greek that originally came from Hebrew? What I am saying is not new to some, and very few scholars would disagree with me on this issue. If there are any who say that the English name *Jesus* was his birth name, then I would ask to see their credentials. Bible scholars know that the name *Jesus* is at least three steps removed from his given name. Unfortunately, most people of faith are not aware of this basic information.

Let's take a simple, yet revealing, journey in the English Bible to expose the truth of the original name of the one called *Jesus.* The first place to look is in the familiar passage in the Gospel of Matthew where the angel tells Joseph what to name his son:

> She will give birth to a son, and you are to give him the name Jesus,* because he will save his people from their sin.
>
> MATTHEW 1:21 (NIV)[206]

---

[206] NIV is the abbreviation for the New International Version of the English Bible.

This verse is at the center of the confusion in more ways than one. Notice the asterisk in the above verse. Open your Bible and see if there is an asterisk or footnote in Matthew 1:21. This small footnote is a key to understanding the name of the one called *Jesus*. Unfortunately, many English versions do not footnote this verse for fear that you might figure out the *trick*.

In the NIV and a few other translations the footnote will lead you to something that says, *"Jesus is the Greek form of Joshua, which means the 'Lord saves.'"* This statement is not accurate. Actually, *Jesus* is a transliteration from the Greek name Ιεσους (*Iesous*). Many Christian and even Jewish people are not aware of these important facts. We will analyze the significance of this name as we proceed, but for now we will focus on the *trickery* practiced by many English translators. The question must be asked, "Why is the name Ιεσους (*Iesous*) sometimes translated as *Jesus* and sometimes as *Joshua?"* The footnote explains that the original Hebrew name corresponds to our English name *Joshua,* and since we know the Greek equivalent of this name, why not be consistent? The name should be translated either as *Jesus* or as *Joshua*, not both.

You can verify the consistency of the translators by checking the New Testament references to the *Joshua* of the Old Testament. Would you agree that if we can find any references to Joshua in the New Testament then his name and Jesus' name should be translated the same since both are identical in Greek? There are *two* references to the man named Joshua, who became the leader of the Israelites after Moses died:

> Having received the tabernacle, our fathers under Joshua [Ιεσους, *Iesous*] brought it with them when they took the land from the nations Elohim drove out before them. . . .
>
> ACTS 7:45

> For if Joshua [Ιεσους, *Iesous*] had given them rest, He would not have spoken about another day after that.
>
> HEBREWS 4:8

Why do so many translators employ this trick? I had to go again to my Grandma Fannie Mae Hayes' old King James Bible in order to find a translation that was consistent on this issue. In both of these verses the King James Version uses the name *Jesus* while most other versions use *Joshua*. In fact, in Hebrews 4:8 the editors footnote the name and explain that this *Jesus* is actually *Joshua*. Are you still with me? Check the above verses in your English version to see if they expose the trick. If not, you should consider getting some other English translations and delay setting this book aside. The question now should be, How do we know that *Joshua* is the source of the name *Jesus?* We must go back in time to understand what happened.

In Chapter Six I addressed the origins of the Septuagint,[207] and how the Hebrew Scriptures were translated into Greek. I encourage you to do your own research on this issue. The short version is that the Septuagint, the "official" Greek translation of the Old Testament, was completed by the Jews of Alexandria approximately 200 years before the first century of the Christian era. This translation is the basis for the way this Hebrew name was translated into Greek.

There is no "sh" sound in the Greek language, so when the Jewish translators came to the name *Yeshua* (Joshua in English), they rendered it as Ιεσους (*Iesous*). Ιεσους is actually a Greek translation of *Yeshu*,[208] a shortened form of Yeshua. When the New Testament was translated into English the translators decided that the best way to render the Greek name would be *Jesus,* except when it refers to the Joshua of the Old Testament. Then most English translators do a *trick* with the name. This was unfortunate since the name *Joshua* is significant, as we will soon see.

The other issue I want to address concerning *trickery* is about one important English letter that has been a major barrier to knowing the name יְהֹוָה Y^{e}hovah and the original Hebrew form of the name *Jesus*. This letter was not even a part of the English

---

[207] The Septuagint is the Greek translation of the Hebrew Bible.
[208] Yeshu was a common Jewish name in the First Century.

alphabet until the fourteenth century, yet knowing the history behind it is a key to understanding the name that has been in existence since the giving of the Torah on the mountain of the One called האל הכבוד הרעים (The El of Glory Thunders).[209]

This famous English symbol is the present-day letter *j*. Any good encyclopedia will tell you that *j* was the last letter added to the English alphabet. Below are *two* witnesses that attest to this historical fact:

> The form of J was unknown in any alphabet until the 14th century A.D., when it originated in the ornamental lengthening of the letter I in manuscripts, particularly when I was an initial letter. . . . However, in the Middle Ages the symbols I and J were used indiscriminately for both the vowel and consonant sound. . . . [T]he capital J is virtually a printer's invention and is something of a makeshift. There is no history attached to this form; there was no Roman model to work from. Like the letter U, it is inferior in design to other letters, lacking the balance, boldness, and dignity of the classical Roman monumental letters.[210]

> J is the tenth letter of our alphabet, and was the last to be added. . . . In the late Middle Ages, when two or more *i*'s were written together, scribes often added a long tail to the last one. Later, the tail was used to indicate an initial I. During the 1600's, an *I* at the beginning of a word was written with a tail.[211]

This *makeshift "printer's invention"* is one reason why the cover-up of Jesus' real name has been so successful.

---

[209] El Hakavoed Hir'im, Psalms 29:3.
[210] David Diringer, "J," *The Encyclopedia Americana International Edition*, vol. 15, page 636.
[211] Marianne Cooley, "J," *The World Book Encyclopedia* (2001), vol. J, page 1.

What shall we call him?

We have been told that we can call him *Jesus, Christ, Savior, Lord,* or any combination of the four. We read in the previous section that there is a connection between the names *Jesus* and *Joshua.* Why is Joshua's name significant? In Numbers 13:8 you will find a man with the name *Hoshea the son of Nun.* He is mentioned again a few verses later when Moses changed his name:

> These are the names of the men who Moses sent to spy out the land; but Moses called Hoshea the son of Nun, Joshua.
>
> NUMBERS 13:16

In Hebrew, *Hoshea* means "He saves." Moses undoubtedly realized that success in the new land could only come through the salvation or deliverance of Y^{e}hovah, not the man Hoshea.

Joshua was the first person in Scripture given a compound name that includes the personal name יְהֹוָה Y^{e}hovah. Moses combined the name Y^{e}hovah with the word *salvation.* Literally, Joshua's name means "יְהֹוָה Y^{e}hovah *saves.* "

In Chapter Eight we saw quite a number of names that start with Yeho- and end with -yahu or -yah. Here are some other names that are compounds of Y^{e}hovah: *Eliyahu* (Elijah), which means "El is יְהֹוָה;" *Yirmeyahu* (Jeremiah), which means "יְהֹוָה establishes;" *Yahezkel* (Ezekiel), which means "יְהֹוָה strengthens;" *Yoel* (Joel), which means "יְהֹוָה is El;" and *Obadyah* (Obadiah), which means "worshipper of יְהֹוָה."

The pronunciation of the name יהושע (Joshua) is a bit easier to explain than the pronunciation of יְהֹוָה Y^{e}hovah. The name appears 218 times in the "Old Testament" and *two* times in the "New Testament." The Masoretes consistently wrote the same vowel points for this name, with only *two* exceptions where the full spelling[212] was used.

---

[212] See Deuteronomy 3:21 and Judges 2:7 where the full spelling (יְהוֹשֻׁעַ) is used.

The Hebrew name of the one called *Jesus* is יְהוֹשֻׁעַ (*Yᵉ-ho-shua*). Take a moment to look at the first Hebrew letter of the names יְהֹוָה Yᵉhovah and יְהוֹשֻׁעַ Yᵉhoshua. It is the letter *yod* י which is the tenth letter of the Hebrew alphabet (remember Hebrew reads from right to left). This letter is often represented in English by the letter *j*. But there is no *j* sound in any of the original biblical languages—Hebrew, Aramaic, and Greek. How then could his name originally have been *Jesus* if the letter and the sound *j* didn't even exist?

There is something else very revealing that even the English translations could not hide regarding this important Hebrew name. It has to do with the context in which יְהוֹשֻׁעַ Yᵉhoshua reveals his name to the apostle Paul. It is interesting that the manifestation was in what Paul calls "a light from heaven." Paul asked, "Who are you?" Let Paul testify to what happened:

> As I was journeying to Damascus . . . at midday . . . I saw on the way a light from heaven, brighter than the sun, shining all around me. . . . I heard a voice saying to me in the Hebrew dialect, "Saul, Saul, why are you persecuting Me? . . . And I said, "Who are you, Lord?" And the Lord said, "I am Jesus whom you are persecuting."
>
> ACTS 26:12–15

Stop for a moment and carefully read what Paul is saying. This is a monumental statement that is essential for understanding the name of the one called *Jesus*. There are *two* words that even our English translations could not hide: "Hebrew dialect." Paul is saying that Yᵉhoshua spoke his name in Hebrew!

Now before you argue with me, take a look at your English Bible. You may have the NIV, which says, "I heard a voice saying to me in Aramaic . . ." Even though Aramaic and Hebrew are close cousins, the Greek text simply does not say *Aramaic*. Even if you do not read Greek, please look at the Greek word that the NIV translated as *Aramaic:* εβραιδι (*Ebraidi*). What does that look like to you? This word should have been translated as *Hebrew.* Regardless of a translator's "anti-Hebrew" bias, you will never find a legitimate translation that will put into Paul's mouth, "I heard a voice saying to me in Greek." There is no such statement! Neither Hebrew nor Aramaic uses the name Ιεσους (*Iesous/Jesus*). We have 218 witnesses in the "Old Testament" as to how this important name is written and pronounced in Hebrew.

It should not surprise you that there are *two* variations of the name Yᵉhoshua. Some people argue that his name is יֵשׁוּעַ *Yeshua.* Others use יְשׁוּעָה (*Ye-shu-ah*) because it is a Hebrew word for salvation. Many people believe that Aramaic was the language of the First Century and that the name יֵשׁוּעַ *Yeshua* is the Aramaic equivalent of the Hebrew Yᵉhoshua.

Besides the Aramaic language argument, there is also strong biblical evidence that the name Yᵉhoshua was written as *Yeshua* during Second Temple times. This supports the belief that over time the long form Yᵉhoshua became the shortened form *Yeshua.* The witness of this name can be found in the post-exilic books of Ezra, Nehemiah, and Chronicles.[213]

The abbreviated form יֵשׁוּעַ *Yeshua* appears 30 times in the post-exilic books. In fact, there is even a reference in Nehemiah 8:17 to "Yeshua son of Nun" (Joshua son of Nun). Most modern English Bible translations will use the name *Joshua* rather than *Jeshua* or *Yeshua* (NIV and NASB). However, there are also *two* examples of the long form Yᵉhoshua (*Joshua* in English) being used in Second Temple times. One is in Haggai 1:14 and the second is in Zechariah 6:11, which proves that the name Yᵉhoshua "survived the exile" and was still used in the long form even during the First Century!

Many names were spoken differently between the First and Second Temple times. *Two* examples are *Yirmeyahu* vs. *Yeremiah* (*Jeremiah*) and *Yeshayahu* vs. *Yesaia* (*Isaiah*). The *yahu* was often dropped when the Israelites were in exile in Babylon and other places. There is good reason to believe that the dropping of the

---

213 See Ezra 2:2, Nehemiah 3:19, 1 Chronicles 24:11, 2 Chronicles 31:15.

"yahu" was because it represented the name יְהֹוָה Y^{e}hovah. In a literal way *Yahu* means "He is Yah!" We have already learned that other nations feared the name and tried to suppress it.

While I was in Israel learning about the name Y^{e}hovah, I found out that Y^{e}hoshua is one of the names that has had the same spelling and pronunciation ever since the time of Moses! I find it amazing that the name has not changed in literally thousands of years. There may have been some who preferred to shorten it, but the proof is that the pronunciation of the name Y^{e}hoshua in the Torah is the same pronunciation in Israel today!

In English there are names like Michael and Elizabeth that are commonly shortened to Mike and Liz. At the time Y^{e}hoshua was born, informal or shortened names like Yeshu and Yeshua were also used. I am certain that when it was time to fill out the official birth certificate at the Bethlehem hospital (probably called something like *Manger Memorial*), it read יהושע בן יוסף (Y^{e}hoshua *son of Yosef*).

Now let's address the issue pertaining to the word *Christ* that is usually added as the second or "last name" of *Jesus*. Is *Christ* the last name of Jesus? Of course not. So where did it come from?

> Simon Peter answered, "You are the Christ, the Son of the living Elohim."
>
> MATTHEW 16:16

The word *Christ* is the English rendering of the Greek word χριστος (*christos*), which in turn is derived from the Hebrew מָשִׁיחַ (*mashiach*). מָשִׁיחַ (*mashiach*), often rendered as *Messiah* in English, means "anointed one" and is a pre-Christian term. Other people, such as Caesar, were given this title before Y^{e}hoshua was ever born. Did you know that in most English Bibles there are only *two* places in the Old Testament where the word מָשִׁיחַ (*mashiach*) is translated as *Messiah*?[214] There are other places where *Messiah* could and should have been used instead of the word *anointed*. However in

---

[214] See Daniel 9:25 and 9:26.

order not to "confuse" or give too much information to Christian English readers, translators decided to reveal the use of the term *Messiah* only *two* times. Dare I bring up that pesky number *two* again?

Please allow me to "confuse you" just a little. Even though the Hebrew Scriptures use the word מָשִׁיחַ (*mashiach/messiah*) 41 times, the English translates the word as *anointed* 39 times.[215] One of the most interesting places this word is used is in reference to the Persian king Cyrus:

> Thus says יְהֹוָה to Cyrus His מָשִׁיחַ [*mashiach*] . . .
>
> ISAIAH 45:1

The Septuagint uses the word χριστω (*christo*), which is the same word used in the New Testament for the English word *Christ*. This means that Cyrus, king of pagan Persia, was יְהֹוָה Yᵉhovah's messiah (Christ). Surprised?

Only *two* New Testament passages actually contain the Greek word μεσσιαν/μεσσιας (*messias*). All the other times—more than 500—the Greek word χριστω (*christo*) is used. However, the most interesting note is found in the following verse in the Gospel of John:

> He found first his own brother Simon and said to him, "We have found the Messiah" (which translated means Christ).
>
> JOHN 1:41

Are you willing to slow down and see what has happened here? The word *Messiah* was directly from a Hebrew source and was translated into Greek, then into English. We have other examples in some English translations where, even though the

---

[215] For example, Leviticus 6:22, 1 Samuel 2:10, 1 Chronicles 16:22, Psalms 28:8, Habakkuk 3:13.

Greek says χριστω (*christo*), the English translates the word as Messiah.[216]

If I open my "left-handed" *Hebrew Gospel of Matthew*[217] I will see *two* of the four references noted earlier using the exact same Hebrew word מָשִׁיחַ (*mashiach*) in the text. Referring to יְהוֹשֻׁעַ (Yᵉhoshua) in Hebrew Matthew 1:16, after mentioning Mary, mother of מָשִׁיחַ (*mashiach*), right after the word "translated" the following word is written out in Hebrew letters, קריסטוס (*christos*). The purpose of this notation was to explain to Hebrew readers that the word מָשִׁיחַ (*mashiach*) had been translated into Greek as χριστω (*christo*).

Now take another look at the verse that started all the confusion. Do you remember the famous verse in Matthew 1:21 that has thrown English Bible readers a curve?

> She will give birth to a son, and you are to give him the name Jesus, because he will save his people from their sin.
>
> MATTHEW 1:21

Here is what it says in the Hebrew Gospel of Matthew (and by now you can probably read the name in Hebrew without my help):

> She will bear a son and you will call his name Yeshua [יֵשׁוּעַ] for he will *yoshia* [יוֹשִׁיעַ, *save*] my people from their sin.
>
> MATTHEW 1:21 (Hebrew Matthew)

This is known as a Hebrew word pun or play on words. The name יֵשׁוּעַ Yeshua connects with the Hebrew word יוֹשִׁיעַ *yoshia*, which means "he will save." Do you see the similarity in form and sound? This indicates that originally this sentence was spoken and

---

[216] See Matthew 1:1, 1:16, 1:17 and 2:4 in the New American Standard Bible (NASB).
[217] Howard, George. *The Hebrew Gospel of Matthew.* Mercer University Press, 1995.

written in Hebrew, *not* Greek, because in Greek the verse makes no sense. What does the name *Jesus* or Ιεσους have to do with *salvation,* which is σωσει *(sosei)* in Greek? Nothing. But in Hebrew, it makes perfect sense, because there is a direct connection between the name and the word *salvation!*

There is also an obvious connection between the names Y^ehovah and Y^ehoshua—they share the same first syllable. Of the 28 manuscripts of Hebrew Matthew that have been uncovered, *two* of them use Y^ehoshua, the long form of the name, rather than the shortened Yeshua.[218] Of course, there are only *two*. In biblical Hebrew the vowels of a name are freely modified. This is exactly what happens with the Hebrew name Y^ehoshua, which means "Y^ehovah saves." This name contains *two* elements, the verb *yoshia* יוֹשִׁיעַ meaning "he will save," and יְהוֹ Yeho-, the first part of the name Y^ehovah. The verb *yoshia (he will save)* is modified when incorporated into the name Y^ehoshua. The *yod* of *yoshia* is dropped and the vowels are modified creating the form -*shua*. The form -*shua* can only exist in a personal name, while the verb form *yoshia* (he will save) would be unusual in a name. For more background information on the topic of Jesus' name in Hebrew Matthew, I highly recommend Nehemia Gordon's booklet titled *The Naming of Jesus in Hebrew Matthew*.[219] I find it ironic that a Jew has written about the origin of the Hebrew name Y^ehoshua/Yeshua, whom Christians call *Jesus,* and that I have written about the origin of the Hebrew name Y^ehovah, whom Jews call *Adonai*. Go figure.

The name Y^ehoshua of Nazareth points to the source of salvation and deliverance, just as it did when Moses gave it to Y^ehoshua son of Nun. Who is the name Y^ehoshua supposed to remind us of—Jesus or Y^ehovah? Who is the One who saves and delivers? I offer the following *two* verses to help you answer this important question:

---

[218] Gordon, Nehemia. *The Naming of Jesus in Hebrew Matthew*. Makor Hebrew Foundation, 2008, page 6.
[219] Gordon, Nehemia. *The Naming of Jesus in Hebrew Matthew*. Makor Hebrew Foundation, 2008.

I, even I am Y^ehovah, and there is no savior besides Me.

ISAIAH 43:11

Yet I have been Y^ehovah your Elohim since the land of Egypt; and you were not to know any Elohim except Me, for there is no savior besides Me.

HOSEA 13:4

There is a crucial fact that all Christians must acknowledge. When Y^ehoshua was standing on that windswept Galilean hillside teaching people to pray, he didn't say, "Hallowed be **my** name." No, my friends, he said, "Our Father in heaven, hallowed be **Your** name," or more accurately, "**Your** name be sanctified," as it is in Hebrew. In fact, I am convinced that he would be confused—even upset—if he heard the many songs and prayers that bless "the name of the LORD" when the worshippers are actually addressing *Jesus* instead of the One whose name he taught us to sanctify. He might either turn over some tables or simply walk out in protest. I guess that is a topic for a different book.

In closing, I have a handful of your favorite candy that I would like to give you. If you can answer these *two* questions, the candy will be yours: *Who is Jesus named after?* and *What does the name Jesus mean?* Y^ehoshua knew the answer. Do you?

Holy Father, keep them in Your name, the name which You have given me. . . .

JOHN 17:11

And I have made Your name known to them, and will make it known. . . .

JOHN 17:26

These are my abbreviated thoughts about the explanation and pronunciation of the name יְהוֹשֻׁעַ (Y^ehoshua). I hope readers will be motivated to do their own research. Just remember there are many people who will perform what I call "linguistic gymnastics" in order to promote a theological agenda. I encourage you to first establish linguistic integrity before you attempt to arrive at theological conclusions. In the end, let the Scriptures give you the truth. May the prayer of יְהוֹשֻׁעַ Yᵉhoshua to his Father יְהֹוָה Yᵉhovah come to pass for all who desire the truth regarding both names:

> Sanctify them in the truth, Your word is truth.
>
> JOHN 17:17

APPENDIX A

PROCLAIM THE NAME

Hebrew descriptions and names of our Heavenly Father
corresponding to the instructional CD
(Attached to the inside back cover of this book)

HEBREW DESCRIPTIONS OF OUR HEAVENLY FATHER

There are four variations of the word *EL* used in this list of Hebrew descriptions:

- EL אֵל GENESIS 14:18
- ELOAH אֱלֹוהַּ ISAIAH 44:8
- ELOHIM אֱלֹהִים GENESIS 1:1
- ELOHE אֱלֹהֵי GENESIS 46:3 This is the word *Elohim* in construct form.

This list can be followed on tracks 2 and 3 of the instructional CD:

1. Eli אֵלִי (My El) EXODUS 15:2
2. HaEl Bet El הָאֵל בֵּית אֵל (The El of the House of El) GENESIS 31:13
3. El Echad Bera'anu אֵל אֶחָד בְּרָאָנוּ (One El Created Us) MALACHI 2:10
4. Elohim Bashamayim אֱלֹהִים בַּשָּׁמַיִם (Elohim in the Heavens) JOSHUA 2:11
5. El Emet אֵל אֱמֶת (El of Truth) PSALMS 31:5 ENGLISH, 31:6 HEBREW
6. El Chai אֵל חַי (Living El) JOSHUA 3:10
7. El Chaiyai אֵל חַיָּי (El of My Life) PSALMS 42:8 ENGLISH, 42:9 HEBREW

209

8. El De'oat אֵל דֵעוֹת (El of Knowledge) 1 SAMUEL 2:3

9. El Elyon אֵל עֶלְיוֹן (El Most High) GENESIS 14:22

10. El Emunah אֵל אֱמוּנָה (El Who Is Faithful) DEUTERONOMY 32:4

11. El Gadol Venora אֵל גָּדוֹל וְנוֹרָא (Great and Awesome El) DEUTERONOMY 7:21

12. El Gibbor אֵל גִּבּוֹר (A Mighty El) ISAIAH 10:21

13. El Gomer Alie אֵל גֹּמֵר עָלָי (El Who Completes for Me) PSALMS 57:3

14. El Gimuloat אֵל גְּמֻלוֹת (El of Deeds) JEREMIAH 51:56

15. El Hakavode Hir'im אֵל הַכָּבוֹד הִרְעִים (El of Glory Thunders) PSALMS 29:3

16. Ha El Hane'aman הָאֵל הַנֶּאֱמָן (The Trustworthy El) DEUTERONOMY 7:9

17. El Hanear'eh אֵל הַנִּרְאָה (El Who Appears) GENESIS 35:1

18. El Ha'oneh Oti אֵל הָעֹנֶה אֹתִי (El Who Answers Me) GENESIS 35:3

19. Ha El Hanoten Nekamoat Li הָאֵל הַנֹּתֵן נְקָמֹת לִי (The El Who Executes Vengeance for Me) 2 SAMUEL 22:48

20. El Elohe Haruchot Lecol Basar אֱלֹהֵי אֵל הָרוּחֹת לְכָל בָּשָׂר (El Elohim of the Spirits of All Flesh) NUMBERS 16:22

21. Ha El Hakadosh Nikdash Bitsdaqah הָאֵל הַקָּדוֹשׁ נִקְדָּשׁ בִּצְדָקָה (The Holy El Will Be Sanctified in Righteousness) ISAIAH 5:16

22. El Kanna אֵל קַנָּא (A Jealous El) EXODUS 20:5

23. Elohim Kedoshim אֱלֹהִים קְדֹשִׁים (A Holy Elohim) JOSHUA 24:19

24. Eli Malki אֵלִי מַלְכִּי (My El, My King) PSALMS 68:24 ENGLISH, 68:25 HEBREW

25. Ha El Ham'azreni Chayil הָאֵל הַמְאַזְּרֵנִי חָיִל (The El Who Girds Me with Strength) PSALMS 18:32 ENGLISH, 18:33 HEBREW

26. Elohe Yisrael Moshia אֱלֹהֵי יִשְׂרָאֵל מוֹשִׁיעַ (Elohim of Israel, a Savior!) ISAIAH 45:15

27. Eloah Mimma'al אֱלוֹהַּ מִמָּעַל (Eloah from Above) JOB 3:4

28. El Mistatear אֵל מִסְתַּתֵּר (El Who Hides Himself) ISAIAH 45:15

29. Elohe Olam אֱלֹהֵי עוֹלָם (Everlasting Elohim) ISAIAH 40:28

30. Ha El Osay Phele הָאֵל עֹשֵׂה פֶלֶא (The El Who Works Wonders) PSALMS 77:14 ENGLISH, 77:15 Hebrew

31. Elohim Ozer Li אֱלֹהִים עֹזֵר לִי (Elohim My Helper) PSALMS 54:4 ENGLISH, 54:6 HEBREW

32. El Nose' אֵל נֹשֵׂא (El Who Forgives) PSALMS 99:8

33. El Shaddai אֵל שַׁדַּי (El Almighty) GENESIS 17:1

34. Elohim Shophtim Ba'aretz אֱלֹהִים שֹׁפְטִים בָּאָרֶץ (Elohim Who Judges in the Earth) PSALMS 58:11 ENGLISH, 58:12 HEBREW

35. El Sali אֵל סַלְעִי (El, My Rock) PSALMS 42:9 ENGLISH, 42:10 HEBREW

36. El Simchat Gili אֵל שִׂמְחַת גִּילִי (El, My Exceeding Joy) PSALMS 43:4

37. El Tsadiq Umoshia אֵל צַדִּיק וּמוֹשִׁיעַ (A Righteous El and Savior) ISAIAH 45:21

38. Elohe Yishi אֱלוֹהֵי יִשְׁעִי (Elohim of My Salvation) PSALMS 18:46 ENGLISH, 18:47 HEBREW

39. Ha El Hagadol Hagibor Yᵉhovah Tsavaoat Shemo הָאֵל הַגָּדוֹל הַגִּבּוֹר יְהֹוָה צְבָאוֹת שְׁמוֹ (The Great Strong El, Yᵉhovah of Hosts Is His Name) JEREMIAH 32:18

40. Veattem adai neum Yᵉhovah ve'anee El וְאַתֶּם עֵדַי נְאֻם יְהֹוָה וַאֲנִי אֵל (You Are My Witnesses, Says Yᵉhovah: I Am El) ISAIAH 43:12

Hebrew Names of Our Heavenly Father

This list can be followed on tracks 4 and 5 of the instructional CD:

1. Anochi Y^ehovah Eloheka אָנֹכִי יְהֹוָה אֱלֹהֶיךָ (I Am Y^ehovah Your Elohim) EXODUS 20:2

2. Ani Y^ehovah Hu shimi אֲנִי יְהֹוָה הוּא שְׁמִי (I Am Y^ehovah, That Is My Name) ISAIAH 42:8

3. B'Yah Y^ehovah Tsur O'lamim בְּיָה יְהֹוָה צוּר עוֹלָמִים (In Yah, Y^ehovah, a Rock Everlasting) ISAIAH 26:4

4. B'Yah Shemo בְּיָה שְׁמוֹ (In Yah Is His Name) PSALMS 68:5

5. Y^ehovah Avinu יְהֹוָה אָבִינוּ (Y^ehovah Our Father) ISAIAH 64:8

6. Y^ehovah Borey יְהֹוָה בּוֹרֵא (Y^ehovah Who Creates) ISAIAH 42:5

7. Y^ehovah Chizkey יְהֹוָה חִזְקִי (Y^ehovah My Strength) PSALMS 18:1 ENGLISH, 18:2 HEBREW

8. Y^ehovah Eli יְהֹוָה אֵלִי (Y^ehovah My El) PSALMS 140:7

9. Y^ehovah Elohe Tsavaoat יְהֹוָה אֱלֹהֵי צְבָאוֹת (Y^ehovah Elohim of Hosts) PSALMS 89:8 ENGLISH, 89:9 HEBREW

10. Y^ehovah EL Olam יְהֹוָה אֵל עוֹלָם (Y^ehovah El Everlasting) GENESIS 21:33

11. Y^ehovah Elyon יְהֹוָה עֶלְיוֹן (Y^ehovah Most High) PSALMS 47:2

12. Y^ehovah Gibbor Milchamah יְהֹוָה גִּבּוֹר מִלְחָמָה (Y^ehovah Mighty in Battle) PSALMS 24:8

13. Y^ehovah Hashophet יְהֹוָה הַשֹּׁפֵט (Y^ehovah the Judge) JUDGES 11:27

14. Y^ehovah Ish Milchamah יְהֹוָה אִישׁ מִלְחָמָה (Y^ehovah Man of Battle) EXODUS 15:3

15. Y^ehovah Izuz Vagibore יְהֹוָה עִזּוּז וְגִבּוֹר (Y^ehovah Strong and Mighty) PSALMS 24:8

16. Y^ehovah Kadosh B'Yisrael יְהֹוָה קָדוֹשׁ בְּיִשְׂרָאֵל (Y^ehovah Holy in Israel) EZEKIEL 39:7

17. Y^ehovah Kanna Shemo יְהֹוָה קַנָּא שְׁמוֹ (Y^ehovah, Jealous Is His Name) EXODUS 34:14

18. Y^ehovah Machsee יְהֹוָה מַחְסִי (Y^ehovah My Refuge) PSALMS 91:9

19. Y^ehovah Melek Olam Vaed יְהֹוָה מֶלֶךְ עוֹלָם וָעֶד (Y^ehovah, King Forever and Ever) PSALMS 10:16

20. Y^ehovah Mifalti יְהֹוָה מְפַלְטִי (Y^ehovah My Deliverer) PSALMS 18:2 ENGLISH, 18:3 HEBREW

21. Y^ehovah Mikkadeshkem יְהֹוָה מְקַדִּשְׁכֶם (Y^ehovah Who Sanctifies You) EXODUS 31:13

22. Y^ehovah Mitzudati יְהֹוָה מְצוּדָתִי (Y^ehovah My Fortress) PSALMS 18:2 ENGLISH, 18:3 HEBREW

23. Y^ehovah Moshiek Vegoalech יְהֹוָה מוֹשִׁיעֵךְ וְגֹאֲלֵךְ (Y^ehovah Who Saves You and Redeems You) ISAIAH 49:26

24. Y^ehovah Nissi יְהֹוָה נִסִּי (Y^ehovah My Sign) EXODUS 17:15

25. Y^ehovah Ori Vayishi יְהֹוָה אוֹרִי וְיִשְׁע (Y^ehovah My Light and My Salvation) PSALMS 27:1

26. Y^ehovah Ro'i יְהֹוָה רֹעִי (Y^ehovah My Shepherd) PSALMS 23:1

27. Y^ehovah Ropheka יְהֹוָה רֹפְאֶךָ (Y^ehovah Who Heals You) EXODUS 15:26

28. Y^ehovah Sali יְהֹוָה סַלְעִי (Y^ehovah My Rock) PSALMS 18:2 ENGLISH, 18:3 HEBREW

29. Y^ehovah Shalom יְהֹוָה שָׁלוֹם (Y^ehovah Is Peace) JUDGES 6:24

30. Y^ehovah Shama יְהֹוָה שָׁמָּה (Y^ehovah Is There) EZEKIEL 48:35

31. Y^ehovah Tsidkenu יְהֹוָה צִדְקֵנוּ (Y^ehovah Our Righteousness) JEREMIAH 23:6

32. Y^ehovah Tsori Vegoali יְהֹוָה צוּרִי וְגֹאֲלִי (Y^ehovah My Rock and My Redeemer) PSALMS 19:14 ENGLISH, 19:15 HEBREW

33. Yᵉhovah Uzi Umagini יְהֹוָה עֻזִּי וּמָגִנִּי (Yᵉhovah My Strength and My Shield) PSALMS 28:7

34. Yᵉhovah Yigmor Ba'adee יְהֹוָה יִגְמֹר בַּעֲדִי (Yᵉhovah Who Completes through Me) PSALMS 138:8

35. Yᵉhovah Yireh יְהֹוָה יִרְאֶה (Yᵉhovah Who Sees) GENESIS 22:14

36. Yᵉhovah Yᵉhovah EL Rachum Vechanun Erek Apieyim Verav Chesed Veemet
    יְהֹוָה יְהֹוָה אֵל רַחוּם וְחַנּוּן אֶרֶךְ אַפַּיִם וְרַב חֶסֶד וֶאֱמֶת
    (Yᵉhovah, Yᵉhovah, El Compassionate and Gracious; Slow to Anger and Great in Love and Truth) EXODUS 34:6

37. Yᵉhovah Shophtenu Yᵉhovah Mechoqtenu Yᵉhovah Malkenu Hu Yoshianu
    יְהֹוָה שֹׁפְטֵנוּ יְהֹוָה מְחֹקְקֵנוּ יְהֹוָה מַלְכֵּנוּ הוּא יוֹשִׁיעֵנוּ
    (Yᵉhovah Our Judge, Yᵉhovah Our Inscriber, Yᵉhovah Our King; He Will Save Us) ISAIAH 33:22

38. Hallelu Yah Hallelu et shem Yᵉhovah!
    הַלְלוּ יָהּ הַלְלוּ אֶת שֵׁם יְהֹוָה (Praise Yah, Praise the Name Yᵉhovah!) PSALMS 135:1

39. Kol Hanishmah tehalel Yah Hallelu Yah
    כֹּל הַנְּשָׁמָה תְּהַלֵּל יָהּ הַלְלוּ יָהּ (Let Everything that Has Breath Praise Yah; Hallelu Yah) PSALMS 150:6

40. Ahalelah Yᵉhovah bechayai
    אֲהַלְלָה יְהֹוָה בְּחַיָּי (I Will Praise Yᵉhovah in My Life)
    PSALMS 146:2

The next two Hebrew phrases can be followed on tracks 6 and 7 of the instructional CD:

Track 6: *Let there be light* Genesis 1:3

וַיֹּאמֶר אֱלֹהִים יְהִי אוֹר וַיְהִי אוֹר
Vaiyomer Elohim yehee or vaiyihee or
(And Elohim said, Light be, and light was.)

Track 7: *Your name be sanctified* Hebrew Matthew 6:9

אָבִינוּ שֶׁבַּשָׁמַיִם יִתְקַדֵּשׁ שִׁמְךָ

Avinu Shebashamayim yeetkadesh Sheemka

(Our Father in heaven, your name be sanctified.)

APPENDIX B

OCCURENCES OF THE VOCALIZED NAME
IN THE LENINGRAD CODEX
B19A

I have referred frequently to the copy of the Leningrad Codex[220] that I possess for my personal study. It is an amazing experience to view the one-thousand-year-old writing of Shemu'el ben Ya'acob, the scribe of this revelatory manuscript. The manuscript was found in the 1800s by Abraham Firkovich, who sold it to the St. Petersburg Imperial Library in the middle of that century. The manuscript is in mint condition despite its age. The letters and the vowels are very clear.

A microfilm copy of the Codex has been available for the past 60 years. A clear photographic copy has been available to the general public for just a little more than a decade. As a result of Soviet Chairman Mikail Gorbachev's policy of *glasnost,* the door was opened for an unprecedented photographic project with the Codex. From May 17 to June 1, 1990, a team of four, consisting of Bruce Zuckerman, photographer and project director; Kenneth Zuckerman, photographer; Marilyn Lundberg, assistant to the photographers; and Garth Moeller, archivist, photographed the manuscript under the joint auspices of the American Biblical Manuscript Center and West Semitic Research Project. This very important Hebrew manuscript contains the following 50 witnesses to the full spelling of the name יְהֹוָה Y[e]hovah and the 49 occurrences of the poetic name יָהּ Yah.

---

[220] For those who are interested, you can download the entire Leningrad Codex here: http://www.seforimonline.org/seforimdb/pdf/264.pdf

Fifty occurrences where the name יְהֹוָ֑ה is fully vocalized and witnessed in the Leningrad Codex B19A:

יְהֹוָ֑ה

Forty-four times the name stands alone with full vowels: Genesis 3:14, 9:26; Exodus 3:2, 13:3, 13:9, 13:15, 14:1, 14:8; Leviticus 25:17; Deuteronomy 31:27, 32:9, 33:12, 33:13; 1 Kings 3:5, 16:33; Jeremiah 2:37, 3:1, 3:13, 3:21, 3:22, 3:25, 4:3, 4:8, 5:2, 5:3, 5:9, 5:15, 5:18, 5:19, 5:22, 5:29, 6:9, 8:13, 30:10, 36:8; Ezekiel 44:5; Nahum 1:3; Psalms 15:1, 40:5, 47:5, 100:5, 116:5, 116:6; Proverbs 1:29.

לַיהֹוָ֑ה

Four times the name is found with the preposition *to:* Exodus 13:12, Leviticus 23:34, Jeremiah 4:4, and Ezekiel 46:13. *To* Y^{e}hovah!

בַּיהֹוָ֑ה

One time the name is found with the preposition *in:* Jeremiah 3:23. *In* Y^{e}hovah!

וַיהֹוָ֑ה

One time the name is found with the conjunction *and:* Genesis 18:17. *And* Y^{e}hovah!

Forty-nine occurrences where the name יָהּ is fully vocalized and witnessed in the Leningrad Codex B19A:

$$\text{יָהּ}$$

Twenty-three times *Yah* is found standing alone or with a prepositional prefix in the Hebrew manuscripts: Exodus 15:2, 17:16; Isaiah 12:2, 26:4, 38:11 (*two* times); Psalms 68:5, 68:19, 77:12, 89:9, 94:7, 94:12, 115:18, 118:5 (*two* times), 118:14, 118:17, 118:18, 118:19, 122:4, 130:3, 135:4, 150:6.

$$\text{הַלְלוּ יָהּ}$$

Twenty-six times in the Hebrew manuscript *Hallelu Yah,* meaning Praise Yah, is found: Psalms 102:19, 104:35, 105:45, 106:1, 106:48, 111:1, 112:1, 113:1, 113:9, 115:17, 115:18, 116:19, 117:2, 135:1, 135:3, 135:21, 146:1, 146:10, 147:1, 147:20, 148:1, 148:14, 149:1, 149:9, 150:1, 150:6.

Bonus Chapter

$$\text{יְהוֹשֻׁעַ}$$

The name Yᵉhoshua is witnessed 218 times in the Hebrew Scriptures and *two* times in the New Testament as *Joshua* (Acts 7:45 and Hebrews 4:8).

APPENDIX C

BOOKS OF REFERENCE

Berkowitz, Ariel, and D. Vorah. *Torah Rediscovered*. Littleton, Colo.: First Fruits of Zion, 1996.

Boman, Thorleif. *Hebrew Thought Compared with Greek*. New York: W. W. Norton, 1960.

Brown, Francis. *The New Brown-Driver-Briggs-Gesenius Hebrew and English Lexicon*. Peabody, Mass.: Hendrickson Publishers, 1970.

Clark, Matiyahu. *Etymological Dictionary of Biblical Hebrew*. Jerusalem: Feldman Publishers, 1999.

Cohen, Abraham. *Everyman's Talmud*. New York: Shocken Publishers, 1949.

Cooley, Marianne. "J," *The World Book Encyclopedia*, vol. J. Chicago: World Book, Inc., 2001.

Diringer, David. "J," *The Encyclopedia Americana International Edition,* vol. 15.

Even-Shoshan, Abraham, ed. *A New Concordance of the Bible.* Jerusalem: Kiryat Sefer Publishing House, 1989.

Freedman, David N., ed. *The Anchor Bible Dictionary,* vol. 6. New York: Doubleday, 1992.

Gaeblein, Frank A., ed. *The Expositor's Bible Commentary,* vol. 3. Grand Rapids, Mich.: Zondervan Publishing House, 1992.

Goldblum Seedman, Terrye. *Holy to Yahveh*. DeBray, Fla.: Longwood Communications, 1966.

Gordon, Nehemia. *The Naming of Jesus in Hebrew Matthew*. Makor Hebrew Foundation, 2008.

Gordon, Nehemia and Keith Johnson. *A Prayer to Our Father: Hebrew Origins of The Lord's Prayer,* Hilkiah Press, 2009.

Greek English New Testament. West Germany: Deutsche Bibelgesellschaft, 1981.

Harper Study Bible. New York: Harper & Row, 1978.

Horowitz, Edward. *How the Hebrew Language Grew.* New York: KTAV Publishing House, 1993.

Howard, George. *Hebrew Gospel of Matthew.* Mercer University Press, 1995.

Jastrow Marcus. *Dictionary of the Targumim, Talmud Bavli, Talmud Yerushalmi and Midrashic Literature.* Judaica Treasury 1971, 2004.

Johnson, Keith E. *For His Name's Sake.* North Carolina: Biblical Foundations Press, 2003.

Josephus, Flavius. *The Complete Works of Josephus.* Grand Rapids, Mich.: Kregel Publications, 1981.

Jouon, Paul, and Muraoka T. *A Grammar of Biblical Hebrew.* Editrice Pontificio Istituto Biblico Rome 2000.

Kalland, Earl S., *The Expositor's Bible Commentary,* vol. 3. Grand Rapids, Mich.: Zondervan Publishing House, 1992.

Kautzsch, E., and A. E. Cowley, eds. *Gesenius' Hebrew Grammar.* Oxford: Oxford University Press, 1988.

Kelly, Paige H. and Daniel S. Mynatt. *The Masorah of Biblia Hebraica Stuttgartensia.* William B. Eerdmans Publishing Company, 1998.

Koster, C. J. *Come Out of Her, My People.* Northriding, South Africa: Institute for Scripture Research, 1998.

Lapide, P. *Hebrew in the Church.* Translated by E.F. Rhodes. Grand Rapids, 1984.

The Leningrad Codex B19A, A Facsimile Edition. Cambridge, UK: Eerdmans Publishing, 1998.

Metzger, Bruce M., and Roland E. Murphy. *The New Oxford Annotated Bible*. New York: Oxford University Press, 1991.

The New Testament in Hebrew and English. London: Society for Distributing the Holy Scriptures to the Jews, 1993.

Owens, John Joseph. *Analytical Key to the Old Testament*. Grand Rapids, Mich.: Baker Book House, 1918.

Perschbacher, Wesley J. *Refresh Your Greek*. Chicago: Moody Press, 1989.

Roxburgh, Gordon. "Trying to Rest," *Apollo 11 Lunar Surface Journal*. http://www.hq.nasa.gov/alsj/a11/a11.posteva.html

Rudolph, Elliger. *Biblia Hebraica Stuttgartensia*. Stuttgart: Deutsche Bibelgesellschaft, 1987.

Tawil, Hayim, and Bernard Schneider. *Crown of Aleppo, The Mystery of The Oldest Hebrew Bible Codex*. The Jewish Publication Society 2010.

The Scriptures. Northriding, South Africa: Institute for Scripture Research, 2002.

Seekins, Frank. *Hebrew Word Pictures*. Phoenix, Ariz.: Living Word Pictures, 1994.

The Soncino Talmud. Brooklyn, N.Y.: Judaica Classics Library, 1991.

The Stone Edition Chumash. Edited by Rabbi Nosson Scherman/ Rabbi Meir Zlotowitz. Brooklyn, New York: Mesorah Publications, 2001.

Tov, Emmanuel. *Textual Criticism of the Hebrew Bible*, Minneapolis, MN. Fortress Press, 1992.

Trimm, James, S., trans. *Hebraic-Roots Version "New Testament."* Hurst, Tex.: Society for the Advancement of Nazarene Judaism, 2001.

Webster's New Collegiate Dictionary, 6th ed. Springfield, Mass.: G. & C. Merriam Company, 1979.

Wilson, Marvin. *Our Father Abraham: Jewish Roots of the Christian Faith*. Grand Rapids, Mich.: Wm. B. Eerdmans Publishing Company, 1989.

Zodhiates, Spiros, ed. *The Hebrew-Greek Key Study Bible, NASB*. La Habra, Calif.: Lockman Foundation and AMG Publishers, 1990.

SCRIPTURE INDEX

Verse numbering follows standard English editions.
Hebrew numbering may be different.